Adventures in
MOSAICS

Adventures in MOSAICS

Creating **Pique Assiette Mosaics** from Broken China, Glass, Pottery, and Found Treasures

Perfect Projects in 4 Easy Steps!

GLOUCESTER MASSACHUSETTS

ROCKPORT PUBLISHERS

MEERA LESTER

MARSHA JANDA-ROSENBERG

First published in the United States of America by
Rockport Publishers, Inc.
33 Commercial Street
Gloucester, Massachusetts 01930-5089
Telephone: (978) 282-9590
Fax: (978) 283-2742
www.rockpub.com

10 9 8 7 6 5 4 3 2 1

Library of Congress Cataloging-in-Publication data available

ISBN 1-56496-999-1

Design: Nina Barnett
Layout and production: *tabula rasa* graphic design
Cover Image and design: Jennifer Wills Photography
All photography by Jennifer Wills, except on pages 9, 10, and 13 by
Rod Humby/www.thejoyofshards.co.uk; and copy portrait photograph
of Raymond Isidore, page 11, by Susan Reynolds

Printed in Singapore

Contents

Chapter One: A Short History of Pique Assiette Mosaics

Mosaic art dates back to antiquity. The ancient Greeks fashioned beautifully decorated pavements working with different colored pebbles. Some can still be seen today in the courtyards of homes on the Aegean Islands. The Romans used the cast-off and irregularly shaped stone chips from sculptors' and masons' yards to create *terrazzo* (stone-chip paving). The North Africans formed simple yet beautiful geometric designs using *tesserae* or chips of stone randomly placed in a mortar base. From ancient times to the present, the basic practice of setting small pieces of stone, glass, or terra-cotta into mortar or plaster hasn't changed much. What has changed is the art itself because it has evolved through centuries of diverse cultural influence, utilitarian need, and artistic vision. Today's mosaics range from classical and functional to idiosyncratic and whimsical. One of the most playful forms of mosaic is shard art or *pique assiette*.

Pique assiette is a popular folk art style in which recycled bits of broken china, glass, ceramic tile, pottery, porcelain, stoneware, and found objects are used to make one-of-a-kind creations. Likely borrowed from an ancient practice of adorning burial sites with pottery and later utilized during Victorian times as an art form in which broken family china and porcelain could be re-created as lovely new pieces of art, today *pique assiette* is attractive to many people from around the world because it recycles materials, is inexpensive to make, and almost anyone can do it.

This surprisingly secular scene is from the chapel wall of Raymond Isidore's *La Maison Picassiette* in Chartres, France.

The Father of Pique Assiette

Raymond Edouard Isidore, a grave-yard sweeper by trade, was driven by a desire to create a sacred space for his spirit and endeavoured to accomplish it through *pique assiette* mosaics. Isidore covered every bare object in his home with *pique assiette* mosaics, including his stove (opposite).

In 1928, a humble graveyard sweeper named Raymond Edouard Isidore (1900–1964) built a small home on 4 acres of land near Chartres, France. Although he did not consider himself an artist, Isidore never-theless felt compelled to adorn his house and courtyard with shards of colored glass and bro-ken bits of pottery that he found on his journeys around the area. He also included in his elaborate designs ashtrays, perfume bot-tles, tea spouts, and other ob-jects that he found in many places, including rubbish piles and quarries. Because Isidore would pick up shards of broken plates and take them to his home, people in his community mocked him, calling him by a derogatory nickname, *Picassiette*. Loosely translated, it means picker or stealer of plates. Others suggest that the name *Picassi-ette* was a play on the name of Picasso and the French word for plate, which is *assiette*. Still others suggest that "plate-scrounger" is more correct. A Frenchwoman I asked translated the name to mean a freeloader or one who shows up for dinner uninvited.

Initially, Isidore collected shards with no particular intention, at-tracted to them as a child might be because of their color and bright sparkle. Later, he attributed his creative endeavor to a drive to create a sacred space — not just a house, but a home for his spirit. After he had covered nearly every square inch of the interior and exterior of his dwelling and all the furnishings, including the woodstove, clock, coffee grinder, and sewing machine, Isidore built a chapel with a courtyard and passages to a retreat house and sculpture garden. His work re-flects recurring and universal themes of religion, death, and the feminine. Whether Isidore was a misfit (as most accounts of his life portray him) or an artistic genius, his home, *La Maison Picas-siette*, stands as his masterpiece and legacy. It attracts tens of thousands of visitors every year.

Pique Assiette *around the World*

Other beautiful large-scale examples of *pique assiette* art abound. In Louviers, France, former milk delivery person Robert Vasseur (1908–) decorated his house, garden, courtyard, fountain, doghouse, and coal shed with mosaic art using shells and broken crockery. In Messina, Italy, Giovanni Cammarata (1914–) created a unique sculpture garden out of shells, pottery pieces, and pebbles in what initially was an attempt to simply display his cement and stone garden art. In Southbourne, England, former coal miner and merchant seaman George Howard (1898–1986) created a house and garden linked by paths and low walls made from shells, broken glass, pebbles, inscribed tablets, and many other objects collected from his travels. In Spain, architect Antonio Gaudí (1852–1926) created many fine examples of this type of mosaic, including the playful balustrade bench for *Parque Güell* in Barcelona. In the United States, Italian immigrant and itinerant worker Simon Rodia (1875–1965) spent thirty-three years making the series of towers known as the Watts Towers, in the Los Angeles suburb of Watts. Rodia used broken pots and bottles, ceramic fragments, glass, and shells. An Indian transport official from Chandigarh named Nek Chand Saini (1924–) began making a small hut and garden for himself in 1958, using reclaimed materials that he found in the dumps of the city. Today his garden and visionary environment span 25 acres and is known as The Rock Garden of Chandigarh.

These are just a few examples of how ordinary people created extraordinary works of art doing what we now call *pique assiette* mosaic. Today, artistic *pique assiette* creations are found everywhere—from garden shops, art galleries, home furnishing outlets, and design centers to wine and art festivals and street fairs.

Detail of a bench created by Antonio Gaudí and decorated by architect and fellow collaborator Josep Maria Jujol in Barcelona's *Parque Güell*.

Getting Started Is Easy

The following is just a partial list of the many decorative *pique assiette* projects you can make for yourself or friends for very little investment in time and materials: stepping-stones, flower pots, bookends, mirror and picture frames, pedestals, clocks, recipe boxes, shelves, umbrella stands, birdbaths, trivets, trays, tables, floor and wall murals, sink backsplashes, doorstops, lamp bases, wall hooks, urns, cement animals, and decorative stones; that's just for starters. Instructions, tips, and caveats for making many of these projects are included in this book. A materials list, an essential tools list, and a glossary of commonly used terms is provided. All you need is your imagination, a base, and some shards to get started. Are you ready? Let's begin.

To start your project, you will first need some shards. Begin by finding some old china pieces, pottery, and tile that you like. Where do you start looking? The answer is anywhere and everywhere. Searching for these items is half the fun.

Searching for Shards

If you have a fascination for other people's castoffs — you know, the kind of stuff you find at flea markets, at white elephant sales at churches, in old boxes at a thrift store, at garage sales in your neighborhood — then you are going to love making *pique assiette* art. Some of the best fun I've had is going off with my girlfriends to scour antique stores and consignment shops to find old dishware that could be turned into shards.

While you will likely do most of your hunting and gathering close to home, imagine doing the same thing on vacation in Europe, Scandinavia, South America, or southeast Asia. Some artists addicted to *pique assiette* travel the world in search of bits and pieces to enhance the beauty of their artistic creations. But you don't need to wait for vacation to get started — begin now. Go to your cupboards

first. There are bound to be dishes that are cracked, cups that you never use, old bowls that you can't bear to toss out. Check your jewelry boxes. Look in the trunks in the attic. Examine dusty boxes in the basement. Don't stop there. Go for a walk in the neighborhood or along a beach. Make sure you have pockets on your shirt or pants. Watch for bits and pieces of shells, colored glass, broken dishware or bottles, and the like. Let your neighbors know what you are doing. You may be pleasantly surprised with an object or two left on your porch. Finally, contact local tile shops. Some will bag broken tiles and sell them at a discount to teachers, artists, and others interested in purchasing defective or broken pieces.

Sorting and Storing by Color

If you don't have a special room to do your art, find a space and set up some shelving where you can stack your flea market finds. For shards and smaller objects, clear plastic craft boxes and large glass jars are great. You can sort your shards by color. You may also want to separate out the bits of colored glass and keep those in separate containers. Ceramic doll heads, animals, drawer knobs or pulls can go in yet another box. The idea is to find a way to organize all your "stuff" so that it will be easy to retrieve exactly what you need by color, pattern, or object.

Choosing Color and Pattern

We choose colors because we like them; something about them resonates deeply within us on a personal level. We also choose colors that serve a purpose or make a statement. Bright yellow says, "bold." Cool blue and green say, "calm." Color can be bright, energetic, jazzed. Or, it can be muted, reflective, and peace-

ful. Certain colors were more popular in particular eras of our history—avocado and gold were the rage the 1950s; pink and black featuring bold designs characterize Art Deco of the 1920s (following the 1925 *Exposition des Arts Décoratifs et Industriels Modernes* held in Paris); and purples, pinks, and leafy greens in ornate motifs inspired by nature typify the era of Art Nouveau of the late nineteenth and early twentieth centuries.

Grouping of certain colors can be also associated with a place. Red, white, and blue are generally thought of as patriotic American colors, and their use in that capacity dates back to the birth of the nation. Other colors might suggest different regions of the United States. For

example, terra-cotta colors, lavender, and turquoise are suggestive of the Southwest, whereas deep greens, grays, and blues might characterize the colors of the Pacific Northwest. Classic blue and white might conjure images of New England along the Atlantic seaboard. Picture shades of azure and cerulean blue and white with a splash of red or vibrant fuchsia, and you might imagine the islands of Greece. Color opposites such as red and green, yellow and purple, and orange and blue evoke images of Provence in the south of France. No wonder the impressionist painters made generous use of these colors that they found in their world. These same colors, when used certain ways in designs and patterns and coupled with brown, white, and black might just as easily suggest motifs in Africa or Mexico. Finally, think of soft shades of sunset colors coupled with the gray-green of olive trees, the darker sap green of

vineyards, and the lemony yellow of citrus groves. Imagine now the colors of terra-cotta, the brown of earth, and the blue of the sea and it's practically impossible *not* to see the Italian countryside. When you examine handpainted Italian dishware, you'll see these colors.

When creating a *pique assiette* work of art, think about the color in the context of place, history, and purpose. It's rewarding to find china patterns from other eras and pair shards of them with tile from the same era. For example, if you found a tile of a geranium that might have been popular in the 1950s, use it as the centerpiece for your art. Surround it with shards of Fiesta Ware plates and cups of the same era to complement. You'll be amazed at how stunning the new creation will look. To create something with a distinctive Asian feel to it, use as the focal point a peony, a flower cultivated for more than 4,000 years

in China. Depending on the color of your peony, try incorporating into your *pique assiette* creation shards of glossy black and clear red, as both colors pair nicely in Asian motifs. A touch of green will further enhance the look. You can create festive south-of-the-border *pique assiette* art by collecting plates or shards in the nationalistic colors of Mexico found in the Mexican flag—green, white, and red. Incorporate sculptural art tiles or pieces of frieze, or objects from the past with pieces of colorful Mexican pottery or dishware. Add in one or more found objects like Mexican silver—a belt buckle, earring, comb, elaborate collar tips, or bollo ornament, even religious artifacts. Old tools, nails, even pieces of mirror increase the interest. In creating these unique *pique assiette* works of art, you are only limited by the boundaries of your imagination.

AMERICA'S POTTERY AND DISHWARE HISTORY IN A NUTSHELL

Majolica, stoneware, and porcelain had already been around for centuries in other parts of the world when, in 1612, colonists in North America began creating bricks and tiles in Virginia and Pennsylvania using baked-clay techniques. In a fishing village near where the colonists first arrived in America, ample evidence has been unearthed that shows the earliest American pottery—earthenware bottles, crocks, and bowls—were yellowware, redware, and salt-glazed or stoneware pottery. Yellowware refers to the color of the clay used to make the pottery. Redware is so named because the iron mineral compounds in the clay cause it to take on a reddish hue after firing. Yellowware weighed less than stoneware and was favored over redware because it was less porous.

Newly arrived immigrants brought pottery with them (artifacts of Staffordshire ironstone china, a utilitarian ware made in the Staffordshire region of England, have been found, as well)

even though a viable pottery industry was already underway in America by the mid-1700s in the area of New Jersey and New York. Rich clay deposits found in that area as well as in Maryland, Ohio, Pennsylvania, and areas in New England meant potteries had ample raw material with which to make their dishware. Many potteries sprang up in response to demand, producing mainly yellowware utilitarian pottery.

Most of the ware produced in East Liverpool, Ohio, was Rockingham ware or yellowware. In 1839, the potters developed whiteware. Though it was not yet comparable to the superb quality of English whiteware, that would soon change, and when it did, East Liverpool would forever be considered by some as the birthplace of the American dinnerware industry. Some of the well-known pottery manufacturers in and around East Liverpool included the Hall China Company (notable for its popular Cameo Rose and Autumn Leaf patterns, both made for the

Jewel Tea Company, as well as many other beautiful patterns), Homer Laughlin China Company (widely known for its Art Deco Fiesta dinnerware and its prodigious output of American restaurant ware), Limoges China Company (highly regarded for its semiporcelain/earthenware china), and Knowles, Taylor and Knowles (recognized by many sources as the first to make whiteware). Rockingham ware continued to be produced in East Liverpool and, by some estimates, between 1865 and 1885, Ohio alone produced half of the America's yellowware.

In Trenton, New Jersey, potters became experts at making delicate Belleek or eggshell china, better known, perhaps, as the type of china created by the Belleek Pottery Company, situated on the banks of the river Erne in Ireland in 1858, and famous for its thin, ivory-colored, glazed porcelain. A number of American companies went on to produce this type of pottery, but because of legal disputes with the Irish, had to cease using the term Belleek. Also, around this time, some American potteries were producing graniteware. Trenton's City Pottery laid claim to being the first pottery in New Jersey to produce "white granite."

By the beginning of the 1900s, the American pottery industry was booming. Other states, including Minnesota, Tennessee, California, and Indiana, to name a few, had either already established dishware production and manufacturing companies or soon would. Many went on to develop unique designs and patterns. Potteries that didn't already have an in-house artist to create patterns and designs to appeal to a buying public, established art departments or arranged to work with outside designers. Soon, independent shops of dishware artists and designers sprang up to fill the need. Professional associations and trade unions to protect workers' rights and to ensure quality of work and production levels also came into being. Inventors were figuring out how to produce more ceramic products using continuous kilns and casting clay into molds instead of fashioning it by human hands. From sanitaryware (tubs and toilets) to bathroom fixtures, tile, and everything else ceramic, needed for the booming home-building going on in the mid-1920s, American potteries' output increased as never before. Soon ceramic dinnerware

was mass-produced and readily available to everyone. Yet, it still seemed that when the occasion called for celebratory, holiday, and otherwise special occasions, our forbears would set their tables with the finest French-, German-, and English-made dinnerware that they could afford. American dinnerware maker, Lenox, was about to change that.

In 1906, roughly five years after he acquired sole ownership of the Ceramic Art Company in Trenton, New Jersey, Walter Scott Lenox founded Lenox, Inc. The company created a superior product that held its own against the European dishware makers. The ivory-tinted, exquisite Lenox china was so prized, it become the tableware of choice for many sitting U.S. presidents and their wives, from Woodrow Wilson to Ronald and Nancy Reagan; the latter's gold-embossed bone china set included 4,732 pieces.

In the mid-1920s, savvy businessmen saw pottery as a potentially popular incentive or promotional item and began offering china pieces as early as 1924 to entice Americans to buy their products. This practice became even more widespread during the Great Depression. Use of pottery and china as an advertising medium also became common practice.

The pottery industry in America flourished at times, and yet, there were also setbacks. In the 1920s, a strike by pottery workers in Trenton, New Jersey, effectively closed down the city's two dozen potteries and brought about the weakening of the trade unions there. Fires, floods, and purchases of potteries by national conglomerates, as well as the return of cheap imports of china from other countries after World War II, sounded the death knell for many domestic pottery companies.

Today, historians, collectors, antique dealers, and individuals eager to find replacement pieces for their own sets, and replacement services are all interested in locating pieces of antique American pottery. Highly prized collectibles include items of yellowware, whiteware, redware, Balleek, white granite, and ironstone, as well as old advertising pieces, such as ashtrays, cups, pitchers, serving platters, and dishes. Increasingly, books are available to help in the search by identifying pieces and their backstamps. An assortment of helpful books includes *Dinnerware of the 20th Century: The Top 500 Patterns,* by Harry L. Rinker (House of Collectibles, 1997); *The Collector's Encyclopedia of American Dinnerware,* by Jo Cunningham (Collector's Books, 1982 with values updated in 1998); and *Encyclopedia of Marks on American, English, and European Earthenware, Ironstone and Stoneware 1780–1980,* by Kowalsky, Arnold, and Schiffer, Dorothy, 1999).

Selecting a Suitable Base

Several types of materials make appropriate bases for *pique assiette* mosaics—wood, metal, ceramic, concrete, and terra-cotta (for example, porous garden pots and saucers). The mastic and grout must adhere to the surface of the base, so it may be necessary to sand hard, nonporous materials like plastic or Formica. It will also be necessary to lightly sand any previously painted or finished wood, especially if it has flaking paint. However, terra-cotta pots, concrete stepping-stones, cement garden animals,

ceramic lamps, and unfinished wood are perfect surfaces for the beginning artist because mastic and grout readily adhere to them. You can make a beautiful birdbath by turning a terra-cotta pot upside down and gluing its saucer to the upturned base. Glue decorative shards, then grout, seal, and place it in the garden where you can enjoy it throughout the seasons.

A word of caution about using wood as a base—anything tiled onto wood will not stand up to moisture or rain, as the wood can expand and contract. When that happens, the tile can pop off and the grout can crack. It is possible to attach backer board on top of the wood with screws and then tile and grout onto the backer board. However, the safest bet for beginners is to keep their wood-base mosaics indoors.

Pique assiette mosaics are versatile. In addition to creating visually stunning yard art and home accents, you will discover how to make unique *pique assiette* mosaics for holiday gift-

giving, seasonal celebrations, and remembrance. Discover the simple joy of creating a new story in art form from little bits and pieces of history—for surely each piece of broken china belonged to some family or person, somewhere, at some juncture in time. Every little shard of pottery had a place in this world before you found it. Each treasure or found object evoked a story or memory in the one to whom the object once belonged. In the recycling and recombining of these pieces into a *pique assiette* mosaic, you, the artist, can give new life, new form, and new appreciation for the collective past of these little pieces.

Glossary of Terms

Adhesive A substance used to bond mosaic materials to a base. Examples include cement, mastic, silicon adhesive, and white craft glue. Thin set, a good adhesive/mortar to use on backer board, can be mixed to the consistency of peanut butter and dries in about an hour. To glue a few loose pieces, you can use a construction glue known as Liquid Nails that dries overnight but is unsuitable for gluing onto vertical surfaces.

Backer board A panel composed of Portland cement and other materials that is water resistant and can be used over wood bases such as a garden table to provide a stable underlayment for the application of mosaic.

Ceramic Heat- and corrosion-resistant materials that are shaped and then fired at high temperatures, making them hard and brittle. Common ceramics include earthenware, porcelain, and stoneware.

Found materials Objects found at yard sales, architectural salvage yards, flea markets, antique shops, recycling centers, second-hand stores, consignment shops, and in home attics and trunks that are desirable for use in creating *pique assiette* mosaics. Found materials include, but are not limited to, buttons, jewelry, figurines, shells, trinkets, knobs, rings, thimbles, porcelain flowers, rocks, marbles, bottle stoppers, drawer pulls—virtually anything the artist feels contributes to his/her art.

Grout Grout is mortar that fills in the spaces between affixed tiles. It can be found in both sanded and unsanded versions. Sanded grout is used to join glass shards, bits of pottery, and broken plates to a base. Unsanded grout, which is finer in texture than sanded grout, is best for applying tiny tiles, less than $\frac{1}{4}$ inch (.5 cm), to a floor.

Interstice The space between each tile, glass shard, or broken piece of china that subsequently gets filled in with grout is called an interstice.

Mastic Premixed adhesive used to attach ceramic tile and glass shards to a base. Mastic has a latex or petrochemical base, dries in 6 to 8 hours, and is easily removed with water from the surfaces of glass and tile when wet. However, to remove when dry requires the use of a scraper and possibly a solvent.

Memoryware Relics of bygone times, including family heirlooms, broken toys, old china, cups, baseball memorabilia, game pieces—virtually anything that evokes personal family memories or remembrance of another era—can be re-created in unique *pique assiette* art.

Pique assiette A folk art style of mosaic that spans various cultures through many time periods, including the Victorian era. Today, *pique assiette* popularly refers to "broken plate" mosaic or shard art. The term *Picassiette,* from the French, was the derogatory nickname given to untrained artist and graveyard sweeper, Raymond Edouard

Isidore, the father of *pique assiette*. For thirty years, Isidore collected shards of crockery and dishware and used them to obsessively decorate his home and garden, *La Maison Picassiette*, in Chartres, France.

Pliers A tool with pivoted jaws used to bend, cut, or hold.

Scorer A tool used to score a straight edge for breaking tile.

Sealer A substance used to seal unglazed or porous tile or grout that might otherwise stain, darken, or discolor.

Shard Shard commonly refers to a piece of brittle substance like glass, china, or metal. A broken piece of pottery may be referred to as a shard but more correctly is called a potsherd, especially if the piece has archaeological significance.

Shardwork Also known as shard art, shardwork is the use of shards or broken pieces of china, glass, ceramic, and/or pottery to create a mosaic work of art.

Smalti Glass covered with metal oxides.

Tessera The basic unit of mosaic pattern, tessera (tesserae, plural) may be any small piece of glass or stone, cut into any shape.

Thin set The use of a thin layer of mortar to bond tiles to a substrate.

Tile nippers A tool used to cut or to break off (nip) smaller pieces from a large shard of tile.

Tools and Materials

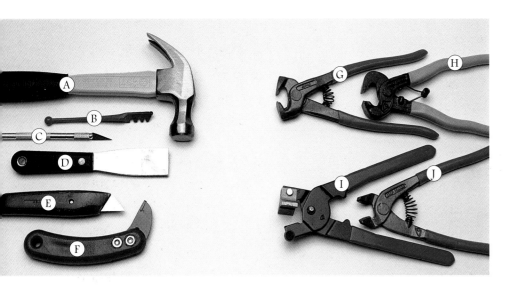

Tools

Essential tools are just that—absolutely necessary to create the art projects in this book. Other tools are included in the list because they are useful but not absolutely necessary.

A. Hammer The hammer is an essential tool for breaking dishware. Always put on safety goggles and wrap the piece of dishware loosely in a towel before tapping it with the hammer.

B. Glass cutter A glass cutter is a useful tool for scoring a straight edge and for cutting glass and tile. Simply mark the line where you desire to cut and then score along the line using even pressure. With the ball end of the cutter, tap the glass gently to break into two pieces.

C. Craft knife This type of craft knife is just what is needed to slice, chip, or scrape away adhesive in unwanted places. For example, scrape away dried adhesive on the top of tiles, where it should not be, or remove an oversized glob that dried in a crack or crevice between tiles.

D. Paint scraper This is one of those useful tools, but it is not absolutely necessary, for when you wish to apply a large amount of tile adhesive to your art and then to smooth it out.

E. Medium utility knife This handy tool works better than the pencil-style craft knife for removing large amounts of dried adhesive.

F. Heavy-duty utility knife This strong utility knife is essential for scoring and cutting backer board or cement board used for murals and any tabletops that are to be exposed to moisture.

G. Tile nipper A tile nipper is essential for creating *pique assiette* art. The nipper is used to cut large shards of china, pottery, and glass into smaller pieces. This is the type of nipper used to create the projects in this book.

H. Tile nipper (variation) Here is a variation of the tile nipper. Use it the same way. Any tile nipper allows for more control in the breaking of large shards into smaller segments whereas a hammer might shatter beautiful motifs or sections of tile or china that you wish to keep intact.

I. Scorer and pliers While not absolutely essential, this tool may be helpful because the pliers has a wheel in the front that allows the artist to score the piece to be cut. Use this tool when a straight cut is needed. Grip the tile with the pliers and simply line up the scoring with the guide mark. Apply firm pressure until the tile breaks along the scoring.

J. Chipper nipper Though not essential to create the projects in this book, this type of nipper is helpful because you can cut circles and shapes that might not otherwise be rendered as well if you used the other nippers shown.

Materials

A. Bucket Buckets are essential; plastic disposable buckets are especially nice because you can mix grout in them and then just toss them when you are finished or allow leftover grout to dry. Then just bang the bucket to loosen the dried grout that can then be dumped and reuse the bucket. Buckets in several sizes are ideal because you'll be mixing varying quantities of grout for different projects.

B. Yellow sponge A large utilitarian sponge is essential for wiping away excess grout.

C. Green scrubber sponges While not essential, these scrubber sponges are handy for gently sanding or scrubbing grout from tile surfaces.

D. Goggles Safety goggles are absolutely essential to ensure that slivers of glass or particles of grout dust do not get into the eyes.

E. Particle mask It is essential to always wear a particle mask whenever you work with grout to avoid inhaling any unseen particles of grout dust, which is harmful to your lungs.

F. Towel A soft towel, like the one pictured, is helpful for dusting and buffing shards once they have been grouted. A heavier terry cloth towel, however, is essential for wrapping dishware to break with a hammer.

G. Latex gloves Wear a pair of latex gloves to apply tile adhesive to shards and to prevent abrasions from sharp edges of shards of china, pottery, and glass.

H. Broom and dustpan These items are helpful to keep your work area clean. Use this size broom and dustpan to sweep away unwanted broken shards, dust and bits of dried adhesive.

I. Rubber gloves Rubber gloves—the durable type you would use to wash dishes—are essential for applying grout to a piece of art covered in broken shards, glass, tile, and pottery. Use them to not only apply grout but also to wipe away excess grout and dust, using the yellow sponge.

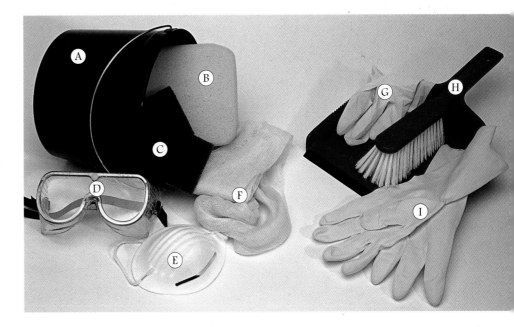

Chapter Two: Four Easy Projects to Get You Started

The beauty of doing *pique assiette* projects is that you don't need a degree in math, a formal knowledge of color and design, or tons of experience as a tile setter to begin playing around with this art form. All you really need to know is the Basic Four-Step Process. Once you learn these easy steps, you can create one of your own *pique assiette* mosaics by following the instructions for any of the four beginner's projects outlined in this section.

THE BASIC FOUR-STEP PROCESS

nippers. Begin arranging your design. If you have a design in mind, you may want to sketch it on paper or directly onto the base, or simply lay out the design upon the base (if it is flat like a stepping-stone). It is often helpful to place the largest design element (centerpiece or focal piece shard) first, and then position the other shards around it to create a pleasing look. The best china pieces for *pique assiette* are those that break where you want them to break. For some types of china, the breakage is difficult to control. The plates don't snap easily and, instead, shatter into small pieces

STEP 1
Prepping
Gather your materials and tools. Choose a base you would like to tile, and select from one to three china pieces to break. Cover the work area in old newspaper. Place the tools, the towel, and the grout within easy reach.

STEP 2
Breaking the Pieces,
Re-creating the Design
Wrap the dish in a towel. Put on safety goggles and protective gloves. Using the hammer, break the dish into large shards. These can later be nipped into smaller, more exact shapes using the tile

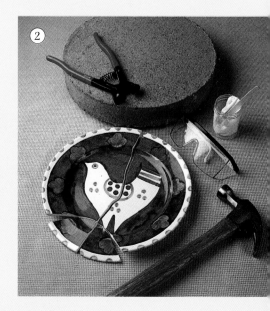

or slivers. Recognizing desirable china for its color and breakability comes with practice. Also, it is helpful to choose dishes that have the design you desire to use located on the flat part of the plate. A design on the ridge or "foot" (located on the back of the plate) will stick out higher than the rest of the plate pieces. Finally, remember that found objects, such as rocks, shells, beach glass, and pottery shards that have washed up on a beach may need a quick spray of clear gloss coating to shine them because grouting will dull the pieces. Apply the gloss and let it dry before proceeding to step 3.

STEP 3
Gluing the Shards

Using a craft stick, scoop up a dab of the premixed mastic and apply it to the back of the shard or tile. Stick the shard onto the base. Continue gluing all the shards onto the base until it is completely covered. Latex gloves may be used for this step because the mastic can dry on the fingers and be an annoyance while you are still arranging and gluing the shards. Remember to let the mastic dry for at least eight hours before applying the grout.

STEP 4
Applying the Grout

Gloves and a filter mask are a must for this step. Wearing gloves and a mask, mix powdered grout (only sanded grout, please) with water until it achieves a peanut butter consistency. Generously spread it over the attached shards until the entire work of art is completely covered. It is important to leave no unfilled cracks, crevices, or spaces. Next, with a damp sponge wipe away excess grout from the shards, tiles, pottery, and found objects. Polish these lovely pieces with a soft towel to allow your chosen bits and pieces to reveal their *raison d'étre*. After your piece has dried for at least twenty-four hours, you may opt to seal it with a tile sealer—several varieties are available at home supply stores. Just douse a sponge with the sealant and make sure you wipe generous amounts of sealant over your piece of art. One other note — it is also possible, prior to applying the grout, to mix an additive into the grout to prevent cracking. Finally, use disposable containers and old towels so you can throw everything away after use. Cleanup is often a messy business.

A couple of helpful hints are appropriate here. First, try to keep the tiles roughly ¼ inch to ½ inch (.5 cm to 1 cm) apart. It gives your finished piece that lovely mosaic look. Wider spacing may result in the grout cracking, especially on wood because wood can expand and contract with temperature and weather changes. This is less so on cement bases. Also, store grout in airtight containers and try to use within six months, as it tends to not mix well and crack more once it gets old.

Playing around with Colored Grout

Sanded grout comes in more than three dozen colors, including seven shades of gray. Basic gray is a good color to use on outdoor pieces because it is already a tone naturally occurring in nature. Colored grout sometimes fades or bleaches out in the weather. Feel free to experiment and mix your own grout color by combining two colors of grout or simply by adding powdered cement coloring. Keep a record of your exact mix to you can re-create it if desired at a later time.

Grout color is a personal choice; however, if you choose a color closely matching your shards, you'll end up with a tone-on-tone look. Instead, think of a background color that complements the main colors of the piece. Just as color choices are important in the selection of shards and tiles for the work of art, grout color is equally important. The best color choices are those that fit the scene. For example, you might use gray grout for an ocean mural that features blue and aquamarine for sea,

brown for palm trees, and beige for sand. A lovely color combination for *pique assiette* is blue and yellow shards against a gray background. The colors seem to just pop.

The first four projects you are going to learn to make include a stepping-stone, a *Bonjour* welcome sign, a decorative saucer, and a tray. A materials list and a set of instructions for each project is given. Refer to the Basic Four-Step Process as needed.

Italian Bird Stepping-Stone

This project is both beautiful and easy to make. You may use a plate similar to this handpainted Italian dish or one that has a large image covering most of the plate. It could be the image of an animal, flower, or fruit. The beauty of this plate is the simplicity of the image and color—a white bird with red markings against a blue background with green leaves. Consider creating a series of stepping-stones, following a theme, to create a small pathway. You might make one for each of the four seasons—winter, spring, summer, and fall—or one for each of your favorite holidays.

Materials List

- dinner plate with a bird or other pretty image
- 12" (30 cm) concrete stepping-stone for a base
- safety goggles
- protective gloves
- towel
- hammer
- nipping tool
- tile adhesive (mastic)
- craft sticks
- particle mask
- rubber gloves
- gray sanded grout
- disposable container
- sponge

Variation Idea

Artist Emily Hammergren enhances the delicate focal image of two flamingos with shards in soft colors—not only on top of the stepping-stone, but around the outer edge as well.

Instructions

2 Break the Pieces

With safety goggles and protective gloves on and the plate wrapped loosely in a towel, begin breaking the plate. Start with a single blow (not too hard as it may shatter the whole plate into so many pieces that it will make it difficult to reassemble them into the original design of the bird). Continue to break judiciously as needed to get large shards; then use the tile nippers to snap off smaller pieces.

Next re-create the design of the bird on the stone so that you'll have a sense of where each shard goes before you begin to apply the mastic.

1 Prepare Your Materials

Following the instructions of step 1 of the Basic Four-Step Process, gather together the materials. For this project, a pretty plate such as this Italian hand-painted bird plate that features a single, strong focal point (the bird) works best. It will be the only art, except for the colored grout, to decorate the concrete stepping-stone.

③

4 Apply the Grout

Put on the particle mask and rubber or latex gloves. Mix a small batch (approximately 1 cup or 250 ml) of gray sanded grout with water. Apply the grout to the tiles and stone, spreading it around evenly. If the stone is a different color than the grout, be sure to rub grout down the sides so that the color matches. Wipe off any excess grout with a sponge and clean up the shards. Buff or polish the shards with a soft terry towel and let the grout completely dry.

You may cover the stone with a sealant before placing it in the garden.

3 Attach the Shards

Starting with the center-most piece, spread the mastic on the back with a craft stick and attach it to the stepping-stone.

Do each piece in turn, working from the center out and then around the entire stone. Allow it to dry, preferably overnight.

Tip

Choose a plate roughly the same size as your stepping-stone to ensure you will have enough shards to fill the border, main focal area, and large empty spaces.

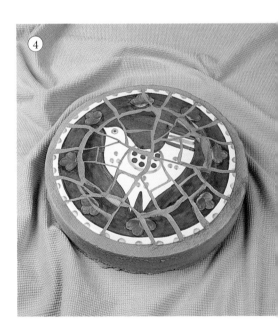

④

Bonjour Stepping-Stone Sign

Bonjour, a lovely French greeting meaning good day/good morning/good afternoon, is a perfect welcome to friends, neighbors, and others who enter your yard or garden. This welcoming stepping-stone sign is both functional and decorative. It may be placed near a doorway or at an entrance to a garden. It can be made in an afternoon and placed in its permanent location the next day. Consider making a name or address plaque for your home, or use a stepping-stone word sign to designate a guest house, doghouse, barn, or potting shed.

Materials List

- shards of yellow, navy, and a two-color (or white/blue) pattern plate
- rectangular stepping-stone for a base
- felt-tip pen
- safety goggles
- protective gloves
- towel
- hammer
- nipping tool
- tile adhesive (mastic)
- craft sticks
- particle mask
- rubber gloves
- gray sanded grout
- disposable container
- sponge

Variation Idea

Notice how the gray grout color recedes allowing this stepping-stone sign's festive colors to send forth a friendly greeting even before you read the Spanish word for hello.

Instructions

1 Prepare Your Materials

To make this stepping-stone, you'll first need to have a two-color patterned plate in a blue-and-white patterned border design, some yellow shards, and navy tile pieces for the word *Bonjour*.

Using the felt-tip pen, draw the letters of *Bonjour* across the center of your stone, leaving equal margins on the left and right and proportional margins at the top and bottom.

2 Break the Pieces

Wearing goggles and protective gloves, place the towel over the two-colored patterned dish and break it into several large pieces with the hammer. Next, nip the large shards in smaller, approximately equal-sized pieces to create a uniform border around the stone. Break a dish to create yellow shards similar in size to those to be used to fill in the space around the word.

Snap a navy dish into shards— make these smaller than the outer border pieces—which will be used to create the letters of *Bonjour*. However, leave four navy shards large enough to nip into squares (roughly the same size as the pieces intended for the border). These four pieces will go into the corners.

3 Attach the Shards

Using a craft stick, spread the mastic on the back of one of the four navy, square corner pieces and set it in place in the uppermost left-hand corner of the stone. Build the border across the top, ending with the second navy square in place in the uppermost right-hand corner. Glue each border shard along the left-hand side of the stone. Place the third navy piece in the bottom right-hand corner and then the fourth piece in the remaining corner. Next, begin gluing the dark, small tile pieces to form the word. Place these close together. Finally, using the yellow shards, fill in the field around the word. Finish the border all around the stone and place more yellow pieces to fill any empty spaces. Allow the mastic to dry.

4 Apply the Grout

The procedure for mixing and applying the grout is the same as in creating the Italian Bird Stepping-Stone. Put on the particle mask and rubber or latex gloves. Mix a small batch of sanded gray grout with water. Apply the grout to the tiles and stone, spreading it around evenly. Remove the excess, using a damp sponge that you frequently rinse in a bucket of water. Buff the shards with a soft terry towel and let the grout completely dry.

As with the Italian Bird Stepping-Stone, you may cover the stone with a sealant before placing it in the garden.

Tip

Gray shades of grout used with black or navy shards tend to dramatize the darker colors since the gray almost disappears into the background.

Italian Bird Plate/
Rooster Saucer

This pretty rooster saucer lends itself to a mission style of house and garden. Use it to show off fruit or vegetables, to serve bread or any dry food items, or display it as an *objet d'art* in your home. Find dishware with any good image of a domesticated animal, such as a pig, cow, horse, goat, duck, or chicken, that might work well, and experiment using the motif and color bands. For a twist, consider lobsters, fish, peacocks, and other images of wild animals that work equally well.

Materials List

- 2 dinner plates—pictured are a Mojave trim plate (circa 1950s) and a Brock ceramic plate featuring a decorative rooster.

- hammer

- nipping tool

- tile adhesive (mastic)

- craft sticks

- goggles

- antique white sanded grout

- medium-sized terra-cotta or clay saucer for a base

- towel

- disposable container

- rubber gloves

- sponge

- particle mask

Variation Idea

In another version of saucer art, a terra-cotta pot serves as a base for Hausenware plate shards featuring images of garden vegetables and chili peppers. A large ceramic chili pepper glued to the edge of the finished pot makes a sculptural statement.

Instructions

1 Prepare Your Materials

A plate with brown/green and yellow trim on a white background and one with a decorative rooster on a white background may be substituted for a similar finished product if you cannot locate the two pieces in the picture. Make sure the plates are roughly the same thickness.

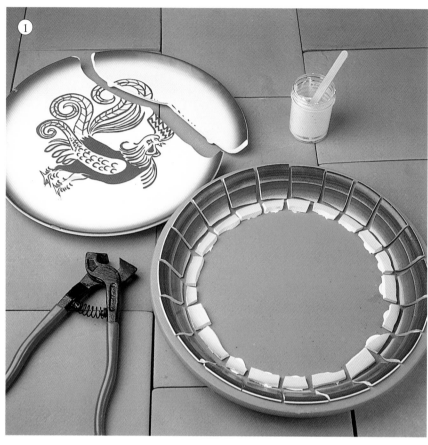

2 Break the Pieces

Next, wearing protective goggles and gloves, wrap the trim plate in a towel and break it. Nip the shards featuring the edge colors into fairly uniform pieces to place around the inside edge of the clay saucer base. Set aside the white center-of-the-plate shards for use later. Next, break the rooster plate. Try to break this plate into as few pieces as possible.

Lay out the pieces in the saucer, re-creating the rooster design in the center of the saucer. Discard the outer edges of the rooster plate. Next, lay the patterned edges of the Mojave trim plate's shards to re-create its pattern along the inner rim of the saucer. The white background pieces will be trimmed with the nippers to fill in the empty spaces.

3 Attach the Shards

Using a craft stick, spread the mastic on the back of each of the border pieces of the Mojave plate and glue them into place. Apply mastic to the rooster pieces and press them into the center of the saucer, re-creating the rooster. These pieces should pretty much fill up any empty space in the bottom of the saucer. Allow the mastic to dry.

4 Apply the Grout

Put on the filter mask and rubber or latex gloves. Mix a small batch of sanded antique white grout with water. Apply the grout to the saucer, filling in all the crevices and wiping away any grout clinging to the pieces you've glued in place.

When the grout work is done, wipe around the edge of the

saucer with a damp sponge to remove any bits of white grout that may be stuck there. Buff the shards with a soft terry towel and let the grout completely dry.

You now have a decorative clay saucer that will serve you for years to come.

Tip

Use a large terra-cotta pot saucer to create a stunning birdbath and a second pot, decorated and turned upside down, as a base.

Decorative Tray

Made from shards of vintage Fiesta-style plates on faux-painted wood, this tray features a bold, circular motif to draw the eye into its artful use of design and bright colors. Perfect for serving lemonade or iced tea on the terrace, it will soon become the focus of the conversation.

Adorned with warm "wake-up" colors, this festive tray could easily become a unique breakfast-in-bed tray for special occasions. For a different design, make this tray reflect that special hour devoted to the taking of tea. Combine favorite broken china shards in the shape of a teapot (or use a teapot image re-created from a broken plate) with uniform pieces of tile to spell out the word *tea, tea shop, tearoom,* or as the French would say, *salon de thé.*

Variation Idea

Artist Theresa Janda shows how to dramatize the circular shape of this tray by following its natural lines in bands of pink-and-yellow china pieces.

Materials List

- 3 plates (various sizes): orange, green, and a plain plate with border of gray-green

- cup with a grape and leaf motif on each side in the colors of orange, green, and white

- 4" × 4" (10 cm × 10 cm) dark green ceramic tile

- rectangular wooden tray for a base

- felt-tip pen

- masking tape

- safety goggles

- protective gloves

- towel

- hammer

- nipping tool

- tile adhesive (mastic)

- craft sticks

- rubber gloves

- particle mask

- Italian straw sanded grout

- disposable container

Instructions

2 Break the Pieces

Next, wearing protective goggles and gloves, wrap the plates in a towel and break each one. Nip the shards into fairly uniform pieces. Set these aside for now, and proceed to carefully break the cup. Try not to break the grape design into more than ten or twelve pieces. The grapes and grape leaves will be the focal point of your tray and will be laid out within the circle. Break the dark green tile and nip the pieces until you have several that are roughly the same size as the plate shards.

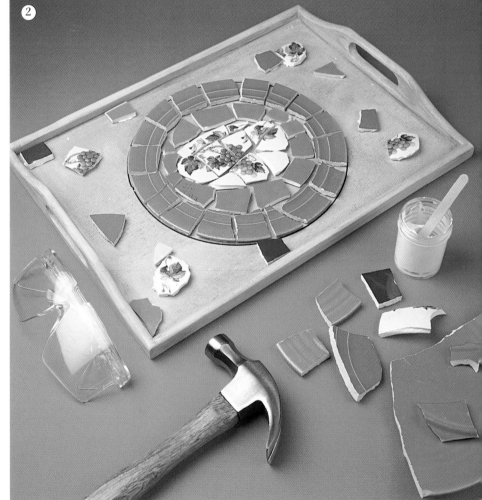

1 Prepare Your Materials

You will need to find a solidly colored orange plate and a green one, plus a plain plate with a border of mint green. You will also need a cup with an image of orange grapes and green leaves. The motif on the cup will become the focal point of your tray. Using a felt-tip pen, trace a circle on the tray (use one of the plates as a guide). Apply masking tape all around the lip of the tray to protect it from the mastic and grout.

4 Apply the Grout

Put on the particle mask and rubber or latex gloves. Mix a small batch of sanded Italian straw grout with water. Apply the grout to the tray, filling in all the crevices and wiping away any grout clinging to the pieces you've glued in place. When the grout work is done, remove the masking tape. Buff the shards with a soft terry towel and let the grout completely dry.

This tray is utilitarian and beautiful. Any size tray may be used. Try making it using holiday-themed china pieces. It may become a family heirloom to be treasured and passed down from one generation to the next. It would also make a wonderful gift for a birthday, retirement, or housewarming. Use broken teapot china to make a one-of-a-kind tea tray. Let your imagination guide you to endless possibilities.

3 Attach the Shards

Using a craft stick, spread the mastic on the back of each of the pieces of the green plate and lay them around the inner ring of the circle. Re-create the grapes-and-leaves design in the middle of the circle, saving four pieces of the grapes and/or leaves to place at each corner. Glue the four saved pieces at midpoints between the green ring and the corners. Next, glue the shards of the orange plate between the grape motif and the ring of green. Glue the dark green tile shards in each corner. Apply mastic to randomly shaped shards of orange and green and mint green and press them into place at the midpoint of each side of the tray. Now fill in with shards of white and color until the entire tray is filled. Allow the mastic to dry.

Tip

Before you glue anything, lay out the mosaic pieces first to make sure that the combination of colors and images is working together to create the look you desire.

Chapter Three: Garden and Yard Art

Nothing provides respite from a busy life like time spent in a garden. Whether it is a tiny portion of earth along the side of an apartment building, an artful grouping of pots on a rooftop, a collection of plants in colorful drifts behind a cottage, a space that offers serenity and quiet along with water (as in a Japanese or water garden), or a grandiose expanse of land sculpted in a formal design as part of an estate or villa—a garden provides a comforting, safe haven. Gardens are so much more than *les fleurs* and *les plantes*. Gardens are places where we dream and allow our imaginations to take flight. They are places where we go to ponder, plan, and even pray. A garden is in the truest sense a *tableau vivant,* a living picture, in which you can add or remove elements to enhance the enjoyment of it.

Some people prefer artistic elements in their gardens, such as arches, gazing balls, stone benches, fountains, topiaries, and statuary, that evoke a more traditional or formal feeling. Others are drawn to less formal, witty, even whimsical garden decorations, including concrete animals, cute little birdhouses, decorative containers, artfully placed rocks, wire-sculpted creatures, movable cut-out characters, and the like. Still others prefer their garden art to include both formal and informal elements. A garden is an ever-evolving work of art, in and of itself. But it is by the addition of personally selected or handmade works of art that the garden becomes an expression of its owner. Garden art—whether formal or informal, traditional or whimsical—is beautified by the addition of *pique assiette* mosaics. Regardless of how your garden appears now, in your mind's eye, visualize what you'd like it to become. Plants are important; design and color are, too, but don't overlook the unique, personal touch that only you can give your garden through your very own creations. Add some *pique assiette* mosaic art into your garden and watch how magical the space becomes.

The next five projects will enliven, enhance, and add color to a garden, porch, potting shed, or yard.

Pot with Italian Shards and Decorative Braid

If you are looking for a stunning foil for the gray-green color of a delicate fern; the yellow tones of a bundle of dried yarrow, common fennel, or yellow rice flowers; or the various shades of brown found in a collection of old wooden-handled gardening trowels, make this pot or a variation of it. Be creative. Try substituting a decorative cup handle, a glass or ceramic fruit or vegetable, or a small ceramic animal such as a frog, hummingbird, or lizard in place of the braid that is shown. The overall effect will be a little different but still lovely.

There are many different approaches to creating a *pique assiette* mosaic design on a pot. A variation of this pot could be made using shards of delicate floral patterns, such as roses, hyacinths, or wisteria, and tiles that have been imprinted with green ferns (you could make these yourself with stencils). Play around with grout colors to see what would best complement your piece. Caveat: Make sure the thickness of the tiles and the china shards are similar; otherwise the end result will be an uneven height for your pieces. One way to circumvent this problem is by placing the thick tile pieces around the top of the pot to form a border and the thinner shards all around the base of the pot. Also consider using pieces of broken mirror, shells that have been sprayed a certain color to complement your pot's color scheme, and other found objects to create texture, beauty, and meaning.

Materials List

- 12" (30 cm) terra-cotta pot that is 10" (25 cm) tall
- miscellaneous Italian pottery with a distinctive Mediterranean look, plus 5 to 6 plates in blue, burgundy, and terra-cotta
- ceramic piece of braid
- gray sanded grout
- hammer
- nipping tool
- tile adhesive (mastic)
- craft sticks
- goggles
- towel
- disposable container
- rubber gloves
- sponge
- particle mask

Instructions

1 Prepare Your Materials

Gather together an assortment of pottery and dishes along with your chosen decorative element (braid, handle, fruit or vegetable, etc.). To get the Italian pottery into smaller pieces, wrap it in a towel before breaking it.

2 Break the Pieces

With safety goggles on, break the Italian pottery while it is wrapped in a towel, then, using the nippers, cut into the shapes you want. Repeat the process for the blue and burgundy plate shards. The blue and burgundy plate shards will need to be fairly uniform in size.

Tip

For foolproof placement of objects onto large terra-cotta pots, first roughly sketch guide marks with a felt-tip pen onto the pot before gluing the pieces with mastic.

Variation Idea

In this variation of art on a terra-cotta pot, you can see how almost any old clay pot can be transformed into a dazzling art object that would look equally beautiful in a garden, sunroom, or windowsill.

3 Attach the Shards

Use the mastic to glue the Italian pottery pieces onto the terra-cotta pot. Re-create the fruit design from the broken shards, keeping the design intact. Glue these pieces onto the pot first, as they will form a focal point. Each of the previously broken Italian pottery pieces had an original border. Find these border pieces and re-create the border on the terra-cotta pot around the lip of the pot and the base. Place the braid in place and glue with mastic onto both the upper lip of the pot and the spot where the bottom of the braid touches the pot's body. Then, add the blue shards to form a ring around the top of the pot under the lip. Use the burgundy pieces to form a ring around the lower part of the pot. Finally, using any extra pottery pieces, fill in the areas that are not yet covered. Let the pot sit undisturbed until the mastic has completely dried.

4 Apply the Grout

Put on the mask before mixing the grout. Using a craft stick, mix the grout with water in the disposable container until it is the consistency of peanut butter. With rubber gloves on, place handfuls of grout over the pot, rubbing grout into all the cracks and crevices. With a damp sponge, wipe away all excess grout. Clean each piece of shard glued to the pot. It may seem a little tedious, but it is a necessary step. Don't forget to use the wet sponge to wipe out any grout from inside the pot. Allow the grout to dry.

The pot is suitable for planting, but do not place in a snowy or perpetually wet area. If the pot is to be placed in a garden, as opposed to a potting shed or garden room, it's a good idea to apply a water sealant all over the pot before putting it in its permanent location. Follow the manufacturer's instructions for applying sealant.

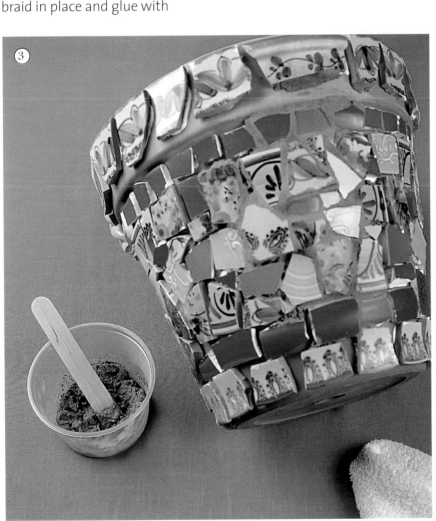

Galvanized Watering Can

Watering cans, essential tools for every garden, are now works of art. You can find them painted with floral designs, adorned with cutout garden prints and patterns and covered with decoupage paste, or tied up with raffia or ribbon and stuffed with pretty silk or dried flowers. By adding some broken Italian pottery and a few plates, the watering can shown here has evolved from a plain old galvanized can into a dramatic *objet d'art*.

Materials List

- galvanized watering can
- 3 Franciscan Desert Rose plates
- 1 green tile, 1 maroon tile
- 6 pink and 6 green marbles (with one side flat) for the handle of the can
- Aspen mint sanded grout
- hammer
- nipping tool
- tile adhesive (mastic)
- craft sticks
- goggles
- towel
- disposable container
- rubber gloves
- sponge
- particle mask

Variation Idea

Instead of a galvanized can, artist Gabrielle Coppel starts with a two-handled decanter and successfully transforms it into a work of art with a distinctive ethnic feel by using unique shards and colors of the Orient.

Instructions

1 Prepare Your Materials

Assemble the dishware, tiles, marbles, and can. Any galvanized watering can will work.

2 Break the Pieces

Wrap dishware in the towel. With safety goggles on, break the dishware into thumb-sized shards. Using nippers, break the tiles into fairly uniform pieces to form two circular bands (see picture) and the decorative lines that gently curve from the top band to the bottom band.

3 Attach the Shards

Use the mastic to glue the dish-ware shards onto the galvanized can, first around the top and onto the spout, then around the bottom. Do not lay the can on its side or rock the can side to side as this will result in the shards dropping off. Glue the solid-colored pieces of tile in place just above the bottom border. Repeat the process for placing tiles just below the top border. Apply the mastic to the flat sides of the marbles and glue them onto the handle of the can.

4 Apply the Grout

Put on the mask to mix the grout. With the craft stick, mix the mint-colored grout with water in the disposable container until it is the consistency of peanut butter. With rubber gloves on, place handfuls of grout over the can, rubbing grout into all the cracks and crevices. With a damp sponge, wipe away all excess grout. Clean each shard that is glued to the can. Use the wet sponge to clean off any grout from inside the can.

If the watering can is to reside in a garden where it will be subject to moisture and temperature variations, it's a good idea to apply a water sealant all over the can. Follow the manufacturer's instructions for applying sealant.

Tip

To achieve a very different mosaic effect, try making diagonals or other geometric patterns up and down the can in contrasting colors, in many different shades of the same base color, or with ethnic images.

Cement Animal

Animals and gardens can go together...or not. If you prefer the animal in your garden never to stalk the birds and leave them as trophies for you to find, dig in your newly planted potager garden, or sharpen its nails on the canes of your prized old rose bush that dates back to 1827, consider an alternative—the cement animal. The cat, pictured here, is an easy project to do and makes a lovely accent for a lush outdoor room or garden. Once you see the striking results, you'll undoubtedly want to make a *pique assiette* menagerie of cement animals, including ducks, frogs, turtles, and birds.

Materials List

- cement or concrete animal
- Taylor, Smith and Taylor rose plate
- turquoise plate
- large, peach-colored dishware shard
- several white dishware shards
- 1 pink marble
- 2 turquoise marbles
- gray sanded grout
- hammer
- nipping tool
- tile adhesive (mastic)
- craft sticks
- goggles
- towel
- disposable container
- rubber gloves
- sponge
- particle mask

Variation Idea

This rabbit, like the cat pictured, is covered with mostly white shards and gray grout; yet it looks very different from the cat because of the addition of china pieces with colorful flower motifs and dimensional roses.

Instructions

1 Prepare Your Materials

Gather together the two dishes, white shards, peach-colored shard, tiles, marbles, and cat. Since the dish with the large rose on it will be broken and reassembled on the cat's back, break the plate carefully so as not to shatter this main image piece.

2 Break the Pieces

Wrap the dish in the towel. With safety goggles on, break the dish into shards. Set aside the pieces of the rose to glue onto the cat's back. Nip any pieces of the rose pattern that are simply too large to fit without having big, protruding edges. Then break the white shards into pieces to be used as filler and also into smaller, uniform pieces that will be used for the base of the cat. Break the turquoise plate and set aside the turquoise-colored shards.

3 Attach the Shards

Use the mastic to glue the rose image onto the back of the cat. Next, apply mastic to the back of the turquoise shards and glue them onto the cat's tail, which is wrapped around the base. Apply the mastic to the flat sides of the turquoise marbles and glue one into each eye of the cat. Next, apply mastic onto the back of the pink marble and glue it onto the cat's nose. Fill in the body of the cat with the white shards, using the peach-colored shards for the cat's paws and ears.

Tip

Use a metal file, Dremel, or heavy-duty sandpaper to remove unwanted grout after it has hardened.

4 Apply the Grout

Put on the mask before mixing the grout. With the craft stick, mix the gray grout with water in the disposable container until it is the consistency of peanut butter. With rubber gloves on, place handfuls of grout over the cat, rubbing grout into all the cracks and crevices. With a damp sponge, wipe away all excess grout. Clean each piece of shard glued to the cat. The cat, if made of solid cement, will be heavy with the addition of mosaic. If the cat is to reside in a garden where it will be subject to moisture and temperature variations, it's a good idea to apply a water sealant all over the cat. Follow the manufacturer's instructions for applying sealant.

CREATING CLAY OBJECTS FOR YOUR *PIQUE ASSIETTE* ART

There are five basic steps to making clay objects for use in your *pique assiette* art. The materials needed include low-fire clay, a rolling pin, a board or flat surface like wood or Masonite on which to roll the clay, a stylus or toothpick to cut desired shapes, a scraper, a baking sheet, artist brushes for applying glazes, and glazing paints in assorted colors. If you use any kitchen utensils such as cookie cutters, cutting boards, baking sheets, and spatulas, etc., keep them strictly for working with clay. Do not reuse them for food.

Basically, there are two methods for making clay objects. One utilizes a kiln and the other uses the standard kitchen oven to bake the clay. Both techniques are discussed here. A word of caution about rolling the clay—if you roll out the clay into thick pieces, there is more of a chance that it might explode or crack during the kiln firing process. Pieces that are too thick may be problematic in creating your mosaic if such pieces are thicker

than the plates and tiles you are using. The surface of the mosaic art will be very uneven. Pieces that are too thin are also problematic because they are hard to handle, fragile in the greenware stage, and as brittle as potato chips. That does not mean they cannot be used, but they must be handled carefully.

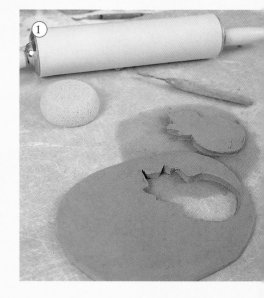

Making Clay Objects Using a Kiln

STEP 1: Cut off a 1- to 2-inch slice of clay from a block of low-fire clay. Lay the clay on a board and roll out with a rolling pin or dowel until the clay is ¼ inch to ⅜ inch (.5 cm to 1 cm) thick. Using a stylus or toothpick, lightly draw your desired shape

and carefully cut along the lines you've sketched. Remove your shape using a clay scraper or metal spatula and place it on a flat surface such as a baking sheet to dry. Reform the excess clay into a ball and once again roll out to ¼ inch to ⅜ inch (.5 cm to 1 cm) thick. Continue to make

pieces until you have as many as you need for the project. Let the pieces dry for three to six days. The amount of time needed will depend on the weather. Clay will dry faster in warm, dry weather.

STEP 2: Apply an undercoat of paint to each piece.

STEP 3: Place on a kiln shelf, insert the shelf into the kiln, and fire to witness cone 04. Bake for approximately seven to eight hours or until the cone slumps and automatically turns the kiln off. Kiln sizes vary and so do firing times. This is also known as bisque firing and renders the piece vitreous (similar to hard glass or stone).

STEP 4: When the pieces are cool, paint with glaze colors or clear gloss glaze.

STEP 5: Fire the painted pieces at witness cone 06. Allow the pieces to bake six and a half to seven hours. When cool, remove from kiln. The pieces, just like purchased tile, are now ready to incorporate into your mosaic.

You can also use cookie cutters to make your shapes, but you will be limited in the types of objects you can make. Press molds (for use in making cookies) may also be used. A handy technique for making leaves is to select a leaf from your garden, press it

into the rolled out clay, then cut around it.

When choosing glazing colors, look at samples of the glaze that have already been fired. Firing may change the color. The temperature for firing clay is usually 2008°F (1098°C) for bisque (cone 04) and 1873°F (1023°C) for glaze (cone 06). Use nontoxic glaze products to eliminate lead contact on your hands. Also, always clean the surfaces used for rolling clay with a wet sponge to remove any traces of clay. Clay dust is harmful if inhaled as it may contain crystalline silica, a chemical known to cause cancer.

Making Clay Objects Using an Oven

If you do not have access to a studio kiln, you can create clay pieces from a type of clay carried in craft stores. Be sure to purchase nontoxic clay that can be baked cement hard in an oven and painted. Such clay can also be sealed to be waterproof. In any case, follow the manufacturer's instructions.

STEP 1: This step is the same as the first step in making clay using a kiln. The clay must be absolutely dry before baking or it may crack, splinter, or disintegrate in the baking process.

STEP 2: Place the clay on an old cookie sheet and slide it into a cold oven. Set the oven temperature to 350°F (177°C) and the timer to one hour. Make sure the room is well ventilated. Higher temperatures are not recommended as smoking may occur.

STEP 3: After one hour, remove clay pieces from the oven.

STEP 4: Let the pieces cool before removing from the baking sheet.

STEP 5: Paint the pieces. Oven-baked craft clay comes out of the oven a warm terra-cotta color that you can paint with a stain, enamel, acrylic, tempera, and terra-cotta color. However, the paint may dull somewhat with the application of grout, and your art may need touch-ups after the grouting is done.

In addition to making vegetables and fruit shapes from clay, try making clouds, insects, letters of the alphabet, clocks, three-dimensional flowers, and faces and body parts. Play around with miniature shapes of musical instruments, cooking utensils, cars and trucks, cowboy boots and stiletto heels, and sports equipment. Don't overlook geometric shapes, architectural shapes, braided shapes, and free-form organic shapes from nature (trees, leaves, Sun, Moon, stars, animals, etc.). Try making slabs with miscellaneous shapes punched into the clay and don't forget miniature articles of clothing like socks, swimsuits, coats, hats, and mittens. Just imagine the possibilities.

Outdoor Mural

Making an outdoor mural requires a little more forethought and planning than the previous projects, but the time and effort is well worth it. For beginners, a simple design is best. Here, the design consists of a palm tree, ocean, sand, sky, and sun. As you experiment with design, try incorporating into your overall picture simple patterns that repeat such as the classic wave-crest (just a little wave with a curlycue top that repeats to make a border) or a large pattern of rosettes (four stones revolving around one center stone). You don't have to limit yourself to a landscape either. Consider the mosaic as you would a painting. By use of color and lines, you can create a mosaic that suggests a bright, bold abstract design or a more conventional composition such as a Victorian vase of cabbage roses. Perhaps you are a sports fan, a gourmet cook, a movie buff, or you know someone who is. Try creating a mural for any of those themes. For children's murals, try remembering your favorite children's stories and allow images to flood your mind. For example, think of a Beatrice Potter children's book, and Peter Rabbit might spring to mind. Imagine a picture of a rabbit and a carrot or a farmer standing by a white fence with a hoe. A mural to adorn a small corner of the garden where children or grandchildren could have a tea party might include Cinderella in a pumpkin carriage, images from favorite fairytales, or children from other lands.

Materials List

- backer board, 20" horizontal × 18" vertical (51 cm × 46 cm)
- 2 shells
- 3 pineapple buttons or small ceramic figures of pineapples
- tiles in the following colors and approximate amounts: 2 green, 4 light blue, 2 medium blue, and 1 dark blue
- 3 "penny" tiles in terra-cotta color (for the coconuts)
- 1 yellow shard
- 3 beige or sandy-colored shards
- green bowl
- brown plate
- turquoise and clear glass marbles with one side flat
- gray sanded grout
- hammer
- nipping tool
- tile adhesive (mastic)
- craft sticks
- goggles
- felt-tip pen
- towel
- disposable container
- rubber gloves
- sponge
- particle mask
- drill and bit to make two screw holes in backer board
- craft utility knife
- sandpaper
- 2 screws
- Optional: Clay accent pieces, such as the pineapples shown. (For instructions on making unique clay pieces for your projects, see the sidebar that begins on page 64.)

Instructions

1 Prepare Your Materials

In your work area, assemble the items from the materials list. With the felt-tip pen, sketch your design right onto the backer board. Round the edges of the backer board by first sketching the curve, then using sharp craft knife or a craft utility knife, trace the curve. Go over it about three times and then, holding the board with the scored back facing away from you, snap away the excess. Use sandpaper to smooth the rough edge. From the center of each upper corner-measure a diagonal line from the corner into the center of the piece. Only go in about 1 to 1 ½ inches (4 cm). Mark this spot in

each upper corner. Drill a pilot hole at this spot in each corner large enough for a screw to fit. Be careful not to shatter the firm texture of the backer board around the hole. Do not cover these holes with tile or mastic. When the mural is finished, you can cover these screws with grout.

2 Break the Pieces

Wrap the green bowl in the towel. With safety goggles on, break the bowl into shards. Set aside the pieces. Break the brown plate. Using the tile nippers adjust the sizes of the dish pieces to fit their purpose. For example, the brown shards will be used as the trunk of the palm tree so you will need eight pieces each slightly larger than the previous one. Next, break the tiles into pieces to create the sea, sand, sky, and leaves of the palm tree.

Tip

Expand your horizons beyond murals. Broken backyard fountains can be repaired with a cement bonding glue and turned into *pique assiette* beauties. Stair steps and concrete walls likewise can be adorned with *pique assiette* mosaics.

3 Attach the Shards

Use the mastic to glue the marbles across the backer board in a pattern mimicking a wave. Position and glue the brown shards for the trunk of the palm tree, working from the base (largest shards) to the top (smallest shards). Apply mastic to the green tile pieces to form the four palm fronds. Using pieces of the dark blue tile, glue them to form a horizon line that meets the center of the palm tree's two fronds that stretch out to the middle of the mural. Piece by piece, continue gluing until all areas are covered except the screw holes. Allow the entire project to dry.

4 Apply the Grout

Put on the mask to mix the grout. With the craft stick, mix the gray grout with water in the disposable container until it is the consistency of peanut butter. With rubber gloves on, place handfuls of grout over the mural, rubbing grout into all the cracks and crevices, everywhere except over the screw holes. With a damp sponge, wipe away all excess grout. Thoroughly clean each marble and shard of dishware and tile. Allow the grout to dry.

If this mural will be placed in a garden where it will be subject to moisture and temperature

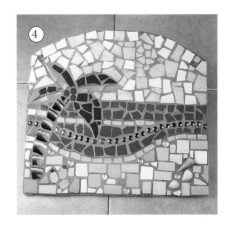

variations, it's a good idea to apply a water sealant all over it. Follow the manufacturer's instructions for applying sealant. When you are ready to place this mural on a wall of a house or on a fence, use a screwdriver to drive the screws through the screw holes and into the wood or stucco. You may then finish the mural by grouting over the screw holes.

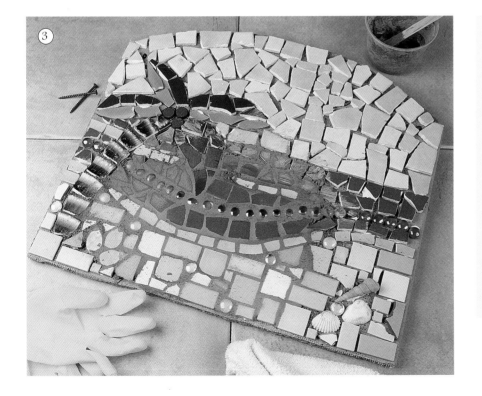

Variation Idea

Murals can be made in all shapes and sizes and feature simple to complex compositions. This particular mural is 4 by 6 feet (1.2 by 1.8 meters) and hangs on the outside wall of a house in California.

Pea Pod Birdhouse

A garden at its apogee is made even lovelier by the addition of a decorative birdhouse. Birdhouses are found everywhere, from garden shops and hardware stores to do-it-yourselfer's warehouses, restaurants, and animal feed stores. They are also easy to make. If you make one from wood, be sure to prime the wood first before applying any mosaic materials. Be advised, however, that wood birdhouses will deteriorate in the rain, even if primed. This one, found in the clearance aisle of a discount department store, is made of aluminum. A small image, also cut from aluminum in the shape of a pea pod, has been glued to the top. This metal birdhouse makes an excellent base for the shards of dishware, and the shiny green marbles are suggestive of large peas.

Materials List

- birdhouse of aluminum or other metal
- brown plate
- white cup with design that suggests garden, birds, or farming tasks (This one features a chicken farmer with a blue trowel.)
- gray sanded grout
- hammer
- nipping tool
- tile adhesive (mastic)
- craft sticks
- goggles
- towel
- disposable container
- rubber gloves
- particle mask

Variation Idea

Vegetable objects can add a bit of whimsy, as you can see on this pig plaque with its carrot pickle fork and asparagus spreader.

Instructions

1 Prepare Your Materials

In your work area, assemble the items from the materials list. Think about how you want to arrange the design pieces onto the birdhouse base before actually breaking any pieces. For this particular birdhouse, the farmer chicken was preserved (by first breaking the cup in sections away from the image of the chicken, then nipping to get the image in the correct shapes to glue close to the right side of the hole). The pattern around the top of the cup was broken with an eye to placing the design at the base of the birdhouse. Caveat: Since this birdhouse is rather small and delicate, lighter-weight cups rather than heavy mugs will work better for breaking into usable shards.

2 Break the Pieces

With safety goggles on and the towel loosely draped to protect you from flying shards but still allowing you to see the cup, use your nippers to make the initial break of the cup. Nip the image area so that it will fit alongside the hole in your birdhouse. Then make two or three breaks across the image. Set aside the pieces and using the towel to wrap the plate, break it with the hammer. Using the tile nippers adjust the sizes of the dish pieces to fit their purpose in your design.

If you have an object such as the small ceramic trowel in this project, save it for use somewhere on the birdhouse such as we have done here. Wrap the brown plate in the towel and break it with the hammer. Then using the nippers, break the brown shards into smaller pieces that you will fit around the entrance and also at random around the back of the birdhouse.

3 Attach the Shards

Use the mastic to glue the cup's border design around the bottom of the birdhouse. Next, glue the farmer chicken or other image close to the hole of the birdhouse and strategically place other pieces on the opposite side of the hole to balance the frontal image. Piece by piece, continue gluing shards of white, yellow, and brown until all areas are covered, making sure to include the ceramic trowel or any other found object to complete the look of your birdhouse.

4 Apply the Grout

Put on the mask before mixing the grout. With the craft stick, mix the gray grout with water in the disposable container until it is the consistency of peanut butter. With rubber gloves on, carefully begin rubbing grout into all the cracks and crevices in the "body" of the birdhouse. Note that the top has no grout and remains the color of the metal base. Thoroughly clean each marble and shard of dishware and tile. Allow the grout to dry.

If the birdhouse will occupy a permanent place in your garden where it will be subjected to moisture and temperature variations, it's a good idea to apply a water sealant all over it. Follow the manufacturer's instructions for applying sealant. Once dry, the birdhouse is ready to hang.

Tip

Cut china shards smaller for tiny birdhouses and add bits of mirror and colored glass to catch the light especially in garden areas where the wind easily moves hanging objects.

Chapter Four: Home Accents

A room that has charm often evokes a visceral response from those who enter it. Whether created around traditional design principles or an eclectic fusion of color, texture, fabric, and furnishings, such a room offers delight for the viewer and reprieve from lackluster similarity. Likewise, a room filled with unusual collections, handmade art, or one-of-a-kind objects inspires wonder and invites aesthetic response. Express the charm of your rooms with handcrafted art that combines purpose with beauty.

In this chapter, you will find objects such as a wall rack with hooks, a mirror frame, a lamp, and an accent table — every-day objects that might be found in any home — transformed into unusual "conversation pieces" that will add interest to any room. Make one or more of these pieces using the same dishware we have used or incorporate plates in the color scheme of the room where your newly created piece will ultimately live. Consider dramatizing a particular piece by choosing floral patterns in bold colors or impressionistic and painterly hues. Play around with black-and-white tile or plates and add a fun splash of passionate magenta, blistering lime, or fiery red. Go for shock value with words found printed on cups or plates. Combine these with intense colors or geometric patterns. Or, if you've collected plates from markets or villages in other lands and want to create a remembrance piece, consider using those. Each of these *pique assiette* home accent pieces has the potential to transform ordinary spaces into extraordinary areas and to add their own distinctive charm to your home.

Wall Rack with Hooks

This indoor wall rack is so utilitarian and attractive, it can be positioned on almost any wall in an apartment or house, including along a hallway or in a kitchen, laundry room, mudroom, living room, kid's bedroom or playroom, guest bedroom, or garden room. Made of china pieces in traditional blue and white, with white grout, the rack works well against most wall colors as well as paneled wood. You can make it using children's broken tea sets or juvenile dishware for colors and patterns that appeal to kids. Or, try creating it in dishware that features giant sunflowers and garden herbs for a country chic look or to hang in your potting shed. Find plates with laundry day motifs or advertisements for soap or bath supplies to make this rack for a laundry room or bathroom. Use dishware featuring seashells, fish, turtles, and water symbols to create a beachcomber look. Just remember that this rack is intended for indoor use only.

Variation Idea

Another way to use blue as a dominant color in a mosaic pattern is to pair it with other primary colors as shown here in this child's bench, created by artist Nori Dolan.

Materials List

- ½" (1 cm) plywood, cut into an 11" × 24" (28 cm × 61 cm) rectangle
- large dinner plate with a blue-and-white checkered border
- medium plate with a dark blue and turquoise plaid against a white background
- medium plate with a turquoise checkered pattern against a lighter shade of turquoise
- white salad plate with an occasional delicate blue pattern around its edge
- white salad plate with a circular blue-and-white motif and a blue border
- sugar bowl lid, white with tiny blue flowers
- 2 ceramic knobs, in a white-and-blue checkered pattern, with screws
- 2 sawtooth picture hangers
- 20 turquoise marbles
- 8 to 10 medium blue marbles
- 6 dark blue marbles
- white sanded grout
- hammer
- nipping tool
- tile adhesive (mastic)
- craft sticks
- goggles
- towel
- disposable container
- rubber gloves
- sponge
- particle mask
- felt-tip pen
- jig saw to cut rectangle into an arch shape; otherwise not necessary
- electric drill
- Optional: disposable pie tins or plastic containers

Instructions

1 Prepare Your Materials

If you desire to have your rectangle shaped into an arch along the top, sketch the desired shape onto the plywood and cut with a jig saw, making certain to follow your sketched lines exactly. Paint the plywood with primer. With a felt-tip pen, make a dot near the bottom of the plywood where you will want your hooks to go. Locate them at least 2 inches (5 cm) in from the sides and 2 inches (5 cm) up from the bottom of the rectangle. Drill a screw hole over each dot. Turn a small saucer or salad plate upside down and lay it flat in the absolute center of the rectangle, then slide the plate straight down toward the bottom edge of the plywood until half of the plate hangs over the bottom of the wood and the other half remains on the plywood. Using a felt-tip pen, trace around the edge of the plate where it is positioned on the plywood. Remove the plate and you will see a half circle. You will place shards in this circle later. Finally, attach the two sawtooth picture hangers at equal distance on either side of the back of your wall rack. On your work surface, place the rest of your tools and materials within easy reach.

2 Break the Pieces

Loosely wrap one piece of dishware in a towel. With safety goggles on and hammer in hand, break the plates one at a time and set aside in disposable containers or pie tins for further cutting. The pie tins allow easy retrieval of similar shards during the gluing stage. When all the plates are broken, use the tile nippers to further cut the blue-and-white checkered plate border into uniform pieces that will define the top edge of your plywood base. Next, use the nippers to refine the shapes of the blue plate with center circular motif. Proceed with cutting uniform shapes from the borders of the rest of the plates. Don't forget to cut the plain white background pieces from the plates as well. Before you start gluing, position a few pieces around the base to be certain that the look is to your liking.

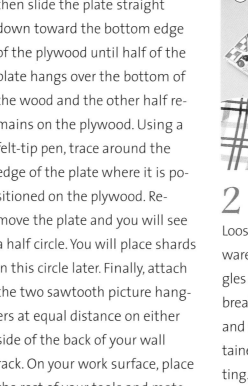

4 Apply the Grout

Put on the particle mask before mixing the grout. Using the craft stick, mix the grout with water in the disposable container. With rubber gloves on, place grout over the wall rack, rubbing the grout into all the cracks and crevices. With the towel, wipe away all excess grout. With a soft cloth, clean each piece of shard.

Attach the knobs with their screws. Now your rack is ready to hold aprons, hats, jewelry, or even dried bunches of flowers tied in raffia or a ribbon.

3 Attach the Shards

Using a craft stick with a little dab of mastic, coat the back of each of the blue-and-white checkered border shards and position them along the top of the plywood. Start at the center and work part of the way left, then return to the center and work around to the right. Take care to space out shards so that you have enough to cover the entire border with even spacing between each shard. Evenly space out the dark blue marbles and glue them into place beneath the checkered border. Do the same for the medium blue marbles. Fill in with the turquoise marbles. Next, glue the shards of the dish with the circular blue motif in the middle. These shards will go beneath the marbles and follow the same line. The plaid plate shards are next. You will need two rows of shards in this plaid pattern. The next step is to use the shards from the blue turquoise checkered plate to fill in the half circle that you drew. Finally, use the shards from the one remaining white plate with the occasional delicate blue pattern on its border to fill in around the top of the half circle. Remember to leave space over the screw holes to allow fitting the knobs in place. Allow everything to dry completely.

④

Tip

Check hardware stores and antique shops for unusual drawer pulls or paint your own.

Picture or Mirror Frame

Who couldn't use an extra picture frame or another mirror in the house? Create this project in woodland motifs or seasonal colors of nature. You could use recycled wood frames or purchase new ones or even make them yourself. This is one project that is cheap and easy to do and looks great when finished. The wood frame shown provides interest with its warm green and yellow color scheme from vintage plates accentuated by an ivy vine in a bottom corner and handmade pressed daisies and yellow flowers along the top. If you prefer softer colors, cover the frame in pale shards, pearly beads, and seashells sprayed in pastel colors. Or, combine vintage shards with uniquely shaped buttons, foreign coins, commemorative pins, colorful stones, miniature ceramic animals, or fruit and vegetables. You might even like incorporating assorted colored glass and mirror shards. Experimentation with different objects can lead to unusual and beautiful creations. So go ahead, dazzle yourself and everyone else who sees the way you've used picture frames and mirrors to accent your home.

Materials List

- wooden 20" × 24" picture or mirror frame
- 2 eye screws and picture hanger wire
- Franciscan Ivy plate
- large vintage plate and one small plate with matching green-and-gold borders
- small vintage plate with two-tone green border and white center
- medium-sized yellow plate with leaf motif around the edges
- medium-sized plate with hash-marked border
- yellow and green odd-shaped condiment dish
- 4 clay flowers in yellow or to look like daisies (see Creating Clay Objects for Your *Pique Assiette* Art on page 64)
- Italian straw sanded grout
- hammer
- tile nippers
- tile adhesive (mastic)
- craft sticks
- goggles
- towel
- disposable container
- rubber gloves
- sponge
- particle mask

Variation Idea

Mirrors are lovely in a garden, as you can see in this photo where artist Anne Spoon-Kanner focuses her mosaics on two pots in an artful arrangement with a mirror painted green. Green is repeated in the china shards as well.

Instructions

1 **Prepare Your Materials**

Gather together the dishware, materials, and tools. Paint the wood frame with primer. When dry, attach the eye screws to the back of the frame roughly one-fourth of the way down on either side. Make the pressed flowers according to instructions given in Creating Clay Objects for Your *Pique Assiette* Art.

2 **Break the Pieces**

With safety goggles on and a hammer in hand, carefully break the matching plates with the green and gold border. Using the tile nippers, nip the shards into pieces that will fit along the edges of the frame. Set these shards aside. Carefully break the Franciscan Ivy plate. Try to keep the ivy motif from being shattered because you will be piecing them together to re-create the image. Set these shards aside. Break the condiment dish in such a way as to preserve one end of it along with a ½-inch (1 cm) or so corner so that once it is attached to the frame, it will look like a small handle. Use the rest of the condiment dish as shards. Break and then nip the hash-mark plate and the two-tone green plate into smaller shards.

3 Attach the Shards

Re-create the ivy pattern along the left bottom side of the frame. Using a craft stick and mastic, glue the ivy pieces. Just above the ivy, position the handle you created from the condiment dish and glue it. Next, glue some of the green-and-gold border shards on the right corner of the frame, extending halfway across and up the frame's edge in both directions from the corner. In the upper right-hand corner glue the four flowers. Using six shards of the leaf pattern, wrap around the upper left-hand corner. With the hash-mark plate shards and the two-tone border plate shards, fill in the remaining empty spaces on the frame.

4 Apply the Grout

Put on the particle mask. With the craft stick, mix the Italian Straw grout with water in the disposable container until it is the consistency of peanut butter. Wearing rubber gloves, place handfuls of grout over the picture frame, rubbing grout into all the cracks. Form smooth edges with the grout. Using a damp sponge, wipe away all excess grout. Clean each piece of shard glued to the frame. Use the wet sponge to clean off any grout from the backside of the frame. When the grout has completely dried, touch up edges in a color such as Old Parchment that matches the grout.

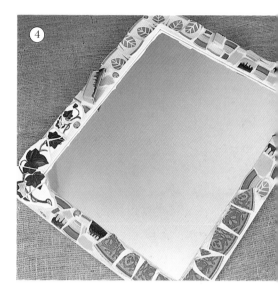

Insert a mirror or picture that has been cut to fit. Thread the wire through an eye screw, twist the wire around itself on one side and then pull it taut. Repeat twisting on the opposite side. Cut off the excess. Hang your art and enjoy.

Tip

While ceramic flowers and seashells make wonderful focal points for mirrors, paint seashells first with clear nail polish to ensure that they don't dull or change colors during the grouting process.

Ceramic Tabletop Lamp

This lamp features Blue Willow shards paired with lemony yellow china in an attractive pattern that combines vertical and horizontal circle motifs. Consider the placement possibilities for this beautiful home accent, as it would certainly enhance any area where illumination is needed. It will look equally lovely sitting on a nightstand, desk, or piano. Or, make two lamps and use them in a formal arrangement on an antique chest or long table in an entryway, atrium, foyer, or wide hallway.

Variation Idea

Here, artist Gabrielle Coppel has achieved a very different look for her lamp using a tall, narrow base and the image of a wild animal.

Materials List

- ceramic lamp with shade
- Blue Willow saucer
- 2 Blue Willow cups
- saucer in blue and white
- yellow cup
- 2 plates with a yellow border and center motif of yellow flowers on a white background
- bright white sanded grout
- felt-tip pen
- piece of paper (8 ½" × 11" [22 cm × 28 cm])
- scissors
- hammer
- nipping tool
- goggles
- towel
- tile adhesive (mastic)
- craft sticks
- disposable container
- rubber gloves
- sponge
- particle mask

Instructions

1 Prepare Your Materials

Gather together the lamp, the dishware, and other materials along with the tools. Using the felt-tip pen, draw a circle onto a piece of paper. You could use a small saucer as a guide. Cut out the circle, position it slightly above center on the front of the lamp base, and trace around it using the felt-tip pen. Make certain that you are drawing the circle on the front of the lamp and that the lamp cord is directly in the back.

2 Break the Pieces

With the towel loosely wrapped around the Blue Willow teacup, use the hammer to break the cup and the Blue Willow plate. Repeat the process for the second Blue Willow cup and the blue-and-white saucer. Set aside these shards and proceed to breaking the yellow cup and plates. Be careful not to hit the plates so hard as to shatter the flowers. You want a clean break. Using the tile nippers, nip the yellow flowers into three or four shards. Make the shards rounded on the edges so that when they are positioned onto the lamp they will form a little circle. Next, use the nippers to nip the Blue Willow pieces into two size groups. One group should consist of fairly uniform shards slightly larger than the second group. The second group of shards will go around the neck of the lamp and will need to be nipped into smaller pieces to fit. Nip the yellow pieces into uniform sizes. Finally, use the nippers to cut the white pieces of china into smaller pieces. You will use these along with yellow shards to fill in empty areas.

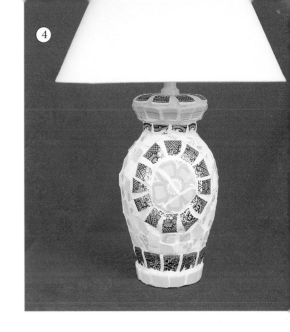

3 Attach the Shards

With the craft stick, use the tile adhesive to glue the yellow flower images in the center of the circle, spacing the three or four shards an equal distance apart. Next, glue the Blue Willow shards in a wider circle around the yellow flowers. On the top of the lamp base and just below and also around the bottom of the lamp, glue solid yellow shards. Just above the yellow border at the bottom, glue Blue Willow pieces. Repeat the process for the smallest part of the neck of the lamp, using Blue Willow here as well. Cover the remainder of the lamp with white and yellow shards. Allow the adhesive to dry.

4 Apply the Grout

Put on the mask. Pour grout into the disposable container and add water until the grout reaches peanut butter consistency. With rubber gloves on, place handfuls of grout over the lamp, rubbing grout into all the cracks and crevices. With a damp sponge, wipe away all excess grout. With a soft cloth, clean each piece of shard. Scrape off any excess grout that gets stuck to the bottom of the lamp. Allow the grout to dry. Polish again.

Tip

Lightly sand ceramic lamp bases before attaching shards with mastic.

Heirloom or Pastel Plates Table

An occasional table is easily transformed into a spectacular accent for your favorite sitting areas. Though not difficult to make, our table suggests by its stunningly good looks that it might have been found in an upscale art and antiques gallery or in the collection of a premier furniture crafter. It may rightly be said of this piece that it is an "accent today, an heirloom to-morrow." Make this table using Grandmother's chipped china to preserve those old beauties in a unique new way, or use plates you find on scavenger hunts. Choose patterns and colors that speak powerfully to you and that will enrich your enjoyment when you use the table. Be exuberant in mixing china plates. Add your own touches of whimsy...or not. Your choices will dictate how a plain table is transformed into a *trés joli table.* Cover it with glass, cut to fit, if you wish to have an absolutely flat surface that can easily be wiped clean.

Materials List

- accent table roughly 20" (8 cm) square
- 6 plates in pastel colors, each with a floral design in the center
- rose-colored salad plate
- felt-tip pen
- bright white sanded grout
- hammer
- nipping tool
- goggles
- towel
- tile adhesive (mastic)
- craft sticks
- disposable container
- rubber gloves
- sponge
- particle mask
- 7 disposable holding containers such as pie tins

Variation Idea

This child's tea table represents just one of the many possible variations for a mosaic tabletop.

Instructions

1 Prepare Your Materials

Gather together materials. Paint the table white, if necessary, to ensure that all surfaces are smooth. Using plates or paper circles as a guide, position them upside down on the table to create the plate pattern arrangement you desire. Trace around the plates with the felt-tip pen to make your pattern.

2 Break the Pieces

Put on the safety goggles. Loosely wrap a towel around the rose-colored salad plate and break it, using the hammer. With tile nippers, nip the large shards into fairly uniform pieces. Place all the pieces into a pie tin or similar holding container. Break all the other plates, in turn, and cut each into smaller, more uniform shards.

Keep each plate's shards in a separate holding container. This will make it easier to re-create the plates, including their borders and floral motifs, during the placement and gluing process.

3 Attach the Shards

From the rose-colored shards, coat the back of one of the pieces, using a craft stick and tile adhesive. Place this shard just inside the circle in the middle of the table. Continue gluing rose-colored shards to complete the circle. Borrow a few shards of flowers from one of the other plates to make an interesting floral image in the center of this circle with the rose shard border. Fill in any empty spaces with white shards. Continue re-creating the plate borders and center floral motifs for all the circles drawn on the table. With leftover white shards, fill in all the space *inside* each plate. With the remaining shards, fill in all the space *outside* of the plates. Allow the mastic to dry.

4 Apply the Grout

With particle mask on, pour white grout into a disposable container. Adding a little water at a time, mix with a craft stick until it is thoroughly mixed to the consistency of peanut butter. Put the rubber or latex gloves on and place a handful of grout onto the table top, gradually covering the surface with grout. Make sure you fill in all crevices and cracks with grout. Dampen the sponge and begin wiping away the excess grout. When all excess grout has been removed, gently wipe each and every piece attached to the tabletop. When the grout has dried, gently wipe each shard again. Touch up table edges with paint, if necessary.

Tip

Paint and repair old tables before applying *pique assiette* mosaics.

Berry Trivet

A trivet is an indispensable kitchen implement. But just because it serves a utilitarian purpose does not mean it can't also be a lovely accent to a kitchen's décor. Use a stone base for best results. While the trivet in the picture incorporates a vine and a lovely raspberry-colored berry motif in the center surrounded by turquoise shards, it also includes a few words from the advertisement on the pitcher used to make the trivet. You may choose to use the words, incorporating them into your artistic creation, or not. Should you opt not to include them, you will have to cut carefully around the berries to separate them from the written material.

Materials List

- stone trivet
- small, white cream pitcher with writing and colorful berries
- white plate with a berry vine design around the border with turquoise, pink, and green colors
- assorted turquoise shards
- rose-beige sanded grout
- hammer
- nipping tool
- goggles
- towel
- tile adhesive (mastic)
- craft sticks
- disposable container
- rubber gloves
- sponge
- particle mask

Variation Idea

Vines add a delicate, lacey look to almost any surface, whether intertwining around the outer edge of a trivet or on top of a cake cover, as pictured here.

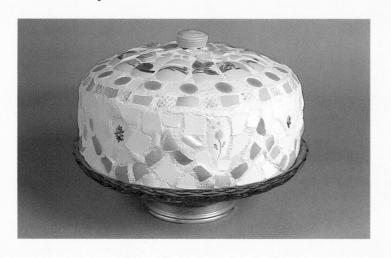

Instructions

1 Prepare Your Materials

Gather together the materials and tools so that everything is within easy reach at your worktable.

2 Break the Pieces

Put on the safety goggles. Loosely wrap a towel around the pitcher and break it, using the hammer. With tile nippers, nip the colorful berries into usable shards for the center of your trivet. Set aside. Next wrap the plate and break it.

Using the tile nippers, cut the plate border into shards of a uniform size to make a border around the edge of your trivet. Cut the white part of the plate and pitcher into smaller shards.

3 Attach the Shards

Using a craft stick and tile adhesive, begin gluing the plate border shards all around the edge of the trivet. Next, glue the turquoise shards inside the circle you made with the border pieces. Glue the colorful berry shards into a small, tight circle in the center of the trivet, and fill in the empty spaces with white shards.

4 Apply the Grout

With particle mask on, pour rose beige grout into a disposable container. Adding a little water at a time, mix with a craft stick until it is thoroughly mixed to the consistency of peanut butter. Put the rubber or latex gloves on and place a handful of grout onto the trivet and begin working it into the surface, fill-

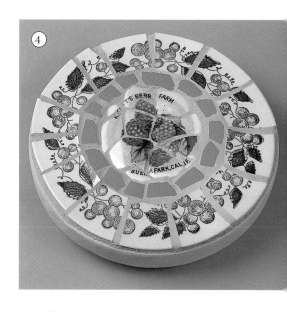

ing all crevices and cracks. Dampen the sponge and begin wiping away the excess grout. When all excess grout has been removed, gently wipe each and every piece attached to the trivet. When the grout has dried, gently wipe each shard again.

Tip

Use flat china pieces instead of sculptured shards anytime you need to have a flat surface, such as for a trivet or coaster.

Chapter Five: Gifts

Nothing says "friendship," "thank you," and "love and appreciation" like a thoughtfully chosen gift. Gift-giving is an art. Those who carefully practice this art consider the recipient and the occasion. Is the gift intended for a cook, an artist, a lover, a grandmother, a boss? Are they newlyweds? Have they moved into a new house, just retired from the company, gone into business for themselves, or celebrating a birthday? Are their tastes conservative, artistic, eclectic? Do they prefer bold, daring colors to softer, more muted tones? Do themes from nature dominate their artistic interests, for example, sunflowers and roosters, or would they prefer art motifs that remind them of travels to other parts of the world? Answers to these questions will help guide you to creating the perfect gift.

The gift ideas in this chapter include four stone coasters, a kitchen utensil caddy, a heart-shaped paperweight, and an umbrella stand. They are all easy to make and are intended to open the tap of your own creative mind. Whether you make just one or all of them, you will soon get a feel for how to think *le cadeau* or gift *à la pique assiette*.

Four Stone Coasters

Materials List

- 4 stone coasters 4$\frac{1}{2}$" (11 cm) in diameter and $\frac{1}{4}$" (.5 cm) thick

- 4 cups or decorative plates (one for each coaster) with pretty images (ours include a blue-and-white teacup image with the Earl Grey name of the tea on a teacup, a Saturnia Italian plate with assorted fruits with green leaves, a golden fish coffee mug along with some shards from a blue-patterned Wildflowers Persian bowl and some smaller shards of an orange floral Asian bowl, and a pink, white, and blue teapot on a plain white teacup.)

- assorted colorful shards to use as borders, if desired

- rose-beige sanded grout

- hammer

- nipping tool

- tile adhesive (mastic)

- craft sticks

- goggles

- towel

- disposable container

- rubber gloves

- sponge

- particle mask

- Optional: 4 felt circles and craft glue to affix felt pieces to the bottom of the coasters

Make all four stone coasters exactly the same for a matched set, or try creating four different coasters. Success will depend on finding the images you seek on dishware. Floral motifs are perhaps the easiest to locate. Coaster bases may be of stone, hard plastic, wood, or glass. To avoid scratches, cut a piece of felt $\frac{1}{4}$ inch (.5 cm) smaller than your coaster base and glue it to the bottom. Caveat: Choose smooth rather than uneven surfaces of dishware to break. If the surfaces of your shards are uneven, glasses and cups may not sit flat upon the finished coasters.

Instructions *(The steps will be the same for each coaster.)*

1 Prepare Your Materials

Gather together dishware, tools, and materials. Smaller pieces will work better since the coasters themselves are small.

2 Break the Pieces

Loosely wrap the dishware in a towel. With safety goggles on and hammer in hand, break the plates or cups one at a time. Carefully cut out the primary image that you desire to use as the focal point of your first coaster. This image will be re-created in the center of the coaster. Set aside the pieces. Using the tile nippers, cut the remaining shards into shapes and sizes to fit the coaster. Try placing the pieces for each coaster on top of the coaster to see how they fit and whether or not a contrast color (such as a border around the coaster) might add interest.

Tip

Choose smaller visual motifs in scale with the small size of a coaster rather than a large image that has to be cut down to fit.

Variation Idea

Hand-cut clay fruits, as seen here in a kitchen wall plaque, could work equally as well when positioned onto a coaster either whole or broken and re-created before grouting.

3 Attach the Shards

Lay out the pieces of the original motif that was on the dishware (the golden fish, for example). In the center of the coaster, re-create the focal image or motif. Next, using a craft stick and mastic, glue each of the pieces in place. Glue the border pieces. Finish by filling in the empty spaces so that you have a pretty mosaic design.

4 Apply the Grout

Put on the mask before mixing the grout. Using the craft stick, mix the grout with water in the disposable container. With rubber gloves on, place grout over the coaster, rubbing the grout into all the cracks and crevices. With a damp sponge, wipe away all excess grout. With a soft cloth, clean each piece of shard. If necessary, when the grout has dried, glue the circle of felt to the base of the coaster.

Repeat the process for each of the remaining coasters.

Roosters and Sunflowers Kitchen Utensil Caddy

What better way to keep wooden spoons, rolling pins, and wire whisks within easy reach than in a utensil caddy? This one can be made in colors to match your kitchen or any interior. Most metal or ceramic containers will work as a base. The pot shown originally came with wire handles, which were removed. The can will be made heavier by the addition of *pique assiette* mosaic pieces and grout; however, if you plan to use it to hold large rolling pins, a taller can that won't tip over might be a better choice.

Materials List

- metal or ceramic can, 6" to 7" (15 cm to 18 cm) tall and 5" (13 cm) in diameter

- 2 rooster-and-sunflower ceramic cups with handles in the shapes of colorful rooster tails

- black-and-white speckled rooster ceramic napkin holder

- 2 red flat-sided marbles

- 2 green flat-sided marbles

- gray-green plate

- red/green Mosaic Fruit Pier One plate

- assorted blue-and-white china shards

- gold-colored saucer shards

- red-colored saucer shards to match color of rooster and Mosaic Fruit plate

- 2 magnets of garden pots with flowers (magnets removed from the backs)

- hammer

- tile nippers

- tile adhesive (mastic)

- craft sticks

- goggles

- towel

- disposable container

- rubber gloves

- sponge

- particle mask

- small piece of sandpaper

Instructions

1 Prepare Your Materials

Gather together the dishware, materials, and tools.

2 Break the Pieces

Put on safety goggles. Using tile nippers, carefully nip one of the cups about ½" (1 cm) from the handle (try not to break the handles). Repeat the process with the second cup. Set the handles aside. Clip the china away to free the sunflowers and rooster images and set them aside. Nip the head from the tail of the rooster napkin ring and set aside. After wrapping the Mosaic Fruit plate in the towel, break the plate with the hammer. Repeat the process with the gray-green plate.

Use tile nippers to cut the gray-green plate into pieces for the top border. Repeat the process for the fruit plate for the bottom border. Nip the other assorted colored shards into smaller pieces for fill.

Tip

For awkwardly shaped shards that have permanent chips, simply touch up the spot with pottery or acrylic paint in a matching color, and you'll never see the chips.

3 Attach the Shards

Use the mastic to glue the rooster tail handles on each side of the can. Next, glue the top and bottom border pieces all the way around the container. Centering the red-colored rooster image in the middle of the can, glue the broken rooster pieces in place. Next, glue a green marble at the spot where the rooster tail leaves off and the top of the handle begins. Above the bottom border in a direct line with the green marble, glue the second green marble. Just above the bottom border under the rooster tail, glue the head of the rooster. Glue the black-and-white rooster's tail near the base of the opposite handle. Below that tail, glue one of the garden pots with flowers. Near the bottom and about 1½ inches (4 cm) toward the rooster head, glue a red marble. Fill in the rest of the area with sunflowers, leaves, and red, yellow, blue, and white china shards. On the center of the back of the pot, glue three sunflowers. Cover empty areas with colored china shards along with green leaves, a red marble, and fruit plate shards. Let the mastic dry.

Variation Idea

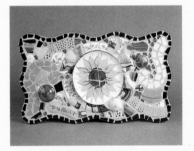

The sunflower motif, ever popular in kitchen and garden art, is shown here in yet another variation, paired with French pottery and sugar bowl lids.

4 Apply the Grout

Put on the particle mask. Add water to the rose-beige grout in a disposable container and stir until it is like peanut butter. With rubber gloves on, place handfuls of grout over the can, rubbing it into all the cracks and crevices. With a damp sponge, wipe away excess grout. Use a sharp object to remove grout from crevices of sunflowers and rooster pieces. Buff each shard. Once the grout has dried, lightly sandpaper off any grout stuck to the inside of the can.

Heart~shaped Paperweight

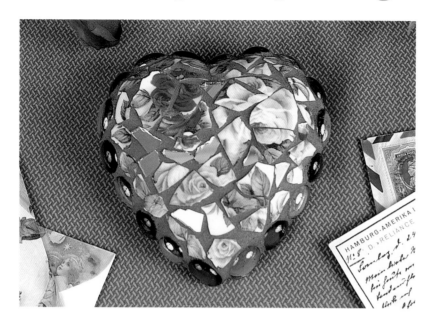

Materials List

- a metal, wood, ceramic, or glass heart-shaped base, approximately 4 ½" × 4 ½" (11 cm × 11 cm)

- rose-covered teacup with red, pink, yellow roses and green leaves

- 7 shards of mirror (roughly ¼" (.5 cm) long)

- 9 red flat-sided glass marbles

- 9 amber flat-sided glass marbles

- gray-green grout (mix one part mallard green with one part winter gray)

- nipping tool

- goggles

- towel

- tile adhesive (mastic)

- craft sticks

- disposable container

- rubber gloves

- sponge

- particle mask

- Optional: one 5" (13 cm) square of red, green, or black felt, scissors, craft glue

Paperweights have been around for centuries. Some sources place them as far back as A.D. 1474 when Venetian glassmakers created intricate floral designs in glass balls. Certainly by the early- to mid-1800s, the popularity of paper-weights reached its highest level. Not only were they utilitarian, but also they were affordable and quite beautiful. Today, paperweights are also quite collectible—the famous Clichy Basket of Flowers sold in 1990 for over $250,000.

You can make *pique assiette* paperweights out of ceramic, metal, wood, or hard plastic shapes that you find pleasing. A wooden egg, found in craft stores, might make the perfect *pique assiette* paperweight for someone at the office who "incubates" ideas. A round glass ashtray can be recycled into a stunning paperweight that says, "Without beginning or end." A square or rectangular paperclip caddy could just as easily become a dazzling reminder of the four corners of the Earth for someone who loves travel. We've used the heart shape to create a romantic paperweight covered with shards of roses and mirror and decorated with amber and red glass.

Instructions

1 Prepare Your Materials

Gather together the rose-covered teacup, heart-shaped base, marbles, and mirror shards along with the other materials you will need from the materials list.

2 Break the Pieces

Put on goggles. With the towel loosely wrapped around the teacup, use the nipping tool to break the cup. Try to protect images of three of the roses (one of each color), so that they do not shatter or break into such small pieces as to be difficult to reassemble on the base. Set aside these pieces and nip the mirror shards into the size that approximates the size of the rose shards.

Tip

Don't be afraid to mix grout to get the color you want, but always write down your recipe so if you have to remix, you will know the proportions.

Variation Idea

Green and pink just seem to go together. Here's another use of china shards with roses. The pink grout keeps the mosaic lines soft while the ornate green stand is a perfect choice as a support.

3 Attach the Shards

With the craft stick and adhesive, glue three rose images onto the top of the base. The red rose goes to the left, the pink to the right, and the yellow toward the lower end of the base. Randomly position and glue mirror and green leaf shards. It makes a nicer image if you re-create an entire leaf or group. At the top center of the heart, place one red marble and next to it an amber marble. Continue alternating marbles around the sides of the heart. Let mastic dry.

4 Apply the Grout

Put on the mask. Pour grout into the disposable container. With the craft stick, mix the dry grout thoroughly. Add water and stir to the consistency of peanut butter. With rubber gloves on, rub grout into all the cracks and crevices. With a damp sponge, wipe away excess grout. With a soft cloth, clean each piece of shard and mirror. Let grout dry. If you like, you can cut a piece of felt into the shape of the heart and glue to the bottom of the paperweight to give it a finished look.

"Tea During Monsoon" Umbrella Stand

People think of umbrella stands as utilitarian, if nothing else. For that reason alone, they make great gifts. During the rainy seasons of the world, they are particularly handy to capture the water that inevitably puddles at the bases of wet umbrellas. Create them to look modern, romantic, delicate, old, rugged, sassy, or even magical.

Our umbrella stand was created with an eye to an Asian aesthetic. Therefore, we used old Chinese coins and bowls, ginger jar shards, and chopsticks, along with bits of mirror, colored glass, and a bird

Materials List

- a glass, ceramic, hard plastic, or galvanized container that stands at least 12" (30 cm) high and measures 6 1/4" (15.5 cm) in diameter (We used an old cracked butter churn, but for umbrellas with long handles, you will need to use a taller container.)

- 2 large plates with a border of light blue with dark blue zigzag lines (ancient symbol representing water) to be used as the top and bottom border pieces

- 3 small Asian condiment dishes with floral borders in the colors of blue, red, green, and apricot to be used as a second border just below the top border

- pale green ginger jar with blue Chinese lettering

- large white plate with a delicate purple, pale blue and soft green floral motif in the center (ours also had gold-trimmed edges and lacey cutout work)

- Rattan Weave Pier One plate

- pale yellow Chinese teacup with green and gray-green bamboo shoots

- several shards of blue-and-white patterned china

- several large shards (can be left over from other projects) in the solid colors of green, gold, blue, purple, and white

- assorted shards from any floral teacups in rose, yellow, green, or blue colors, including any floral-covered handle pieces

- piece of Italian pottery featuring a blue flower with green leaves on a white background round white ceramic lid

- blue-and-green ceramic lid with blue knob on top

- green metal fish-shaped bottle opener

- wooden decorative blue bird with white neck and breast

- 3 blue-and-white ceramic chopsticks holder (one in the shape of a blue fish with a white tail)

- 2 black-and-bone chopstick holders

- 3 pieces of 3/4" (2 cm) square tile in pink, brown, red, and green

- 3 old Chinese coins

- 8 assorted silver buttons one inch in diameter

and fish in mostly quiet colors with an occasional brightly colored piece of glass as a counterpoint for balance. Most of these items can be bought at a discount import shops and craft stores for very little money. Several large shards of English china, which were included in this piece, came from a dinner party where the hostess dropped her gold-edged, scalloped plate. The English plate, with its delicate floral pattern and lacey cutouts, makes a nice foil for all the Asian patterns in this particular mosaic.

The person for whom this umbrella stand was intended spent time in England, and also in the China, Burma, and India theaters of World War II. While the pieces aren't originals from that era, the shards of china used might evoke memories for the recipient of time spent there. One could just as easily target a different generation, choosing objects and colors that represent virtually any era, event, or moment in history. For memoryware, the best objects may be cast-offs items from the life of the person for whom the umbrella stand is intended.

This umbrella stand requires lots of different bits and pieces. If you cannot find exact pieces to replicate this umbrella stand, feel free to substitute others. With *pique assiette*, the idea is to use whatever you can find—that's why it's so much fun to make these projects. Every piece will be unique.

Materials List *continued*

- red flat-sided marble
- 4 blue flat-sided marbles
- 2 green-flat-sided marbles
- turquoise flat-sided marble
- 2 gold flat-sided marbles
- 2 yellow mottled flat-sided marbles
- four $\frac{1}{4}$" (.5 cm) squares of colored glass— 2 blue, 1 yellow, 1 orange
- 8 shards of mirror (roughly 1" (3 cm) long by $\frac{1}{2}$" to $\frac{3}{4}$" (1 cm to 2 cm) wide)

- masking tape
- pale mauve grout
- hammer
- nipping tool
- goggles
- towel
- tile adhesive (mastic)
- craft sticks

- disposable container
- rubber gloves
- sponge
- particle mask
- Optional: 10 to 12 sandwich-size plastic storage containers to hold shards
- Optional: rotating surface (like a lazy Susan) that can spin around

Variation Idea

The long, cylindrical shape of this mailbox is not much different from the upright umbrella stand; however, artist Emily Hammergren has worked textural magic of a different kind on her mailbox, using lots of sculptural pieces and a dusting of sand.

Instructions

1 Prepare Your Materials

Gather together the materials listed. If you've already been making other *pique assiette* projects, you can use any leftover pieces in this project. The mauve grout can be found at tile shops or at discount warehouse stores for do-it-yourself homeowners. The umbrella stand will be heavy, especially as you attach glued items and grout. To make your work easier and to avoid risking breaking off pieces when you turn it, place it on the top and center of a rotating surface like a condiment server that has been covered with newspaper or a dishtowel.

Since there are quite a few materials to use in this project, an important step will be to presort all the materials and place them into pie tins or plastic storage containers (such as those used to refrigerate sandwiches or leftovers). For example, put the marbles, mirror, and pieces of colored glass in one container, the buttons in a second container, and the animals and chopsticks holders in a third. As you break the plates, jars, and bowls, place their shards into containers as well. Keep these containers positioned in a neat row within reach. Having the pieces organized will make it more efficient for you to easily retrieve specific pieces.

2 Break the Pieces

Put on the safety goggles. Loosely wrap a towel around the first plate with the blue zigzag border and break it with the hammer. Set aside the large shards and break the second plate. With the tile nippers, cut the large shards from both plates into smaller, more uniform pieces. Our umbrella stand required twenty-three shards for the top border and nineteen for the bottom. Using the towel and hammer, gently tap—so as not to shatter or fracture the pieces—break the three Asian condiment dishes with floral borders. Use the tile nippers to reduce the decorative shards into smaller, more uniform pieces. Break the ginger jar and nip the shards into smaller pieces. Break the scalloped white plate with the primary image that will appear front and center of your umbrella stand. If the shards need to be cut smaller or the edges need trimming, do the cutting with the tile nippers. Turn your attention now to the Rattan Weave plate. Repeat the steps for breaking the plate and nipping the shards into smaller pieces. Do the same with the pale yellow Chinese teacup with bamboo shoots. Finally, adjust the size, if necessary, of all the mixed shards in the solid colors of green, gold, blue, purple, and white. Also nip the mirror shards, the blue-and-white patterned china shards, and any floral teacup shards into appropriate sizes for random placement in the mosaic design.

3 Attach the Shards

Initially, you will be gluing several key pieces into place. Once they are attached to the base, you will have points of departure around which you can randomly add the remaining shards, mirrors, marbles, and glass.

With the craft stick, use the tile adhesive to glue the top and bottom borders of the umbrella stand, using the blue zigzag shards. Try to space the shards equally for a nice mosaic look. In the center of the front of your umbrella stand, glue the blue fish chopstick holder at an angle right beneath the base of the top border. Create a second border by using shards of the Asian condiment bowls. Start this second border at the fish chopstick holder and continue around until you are back to the fish. Right below the blue fish chopstick holder, slightly above dead center on your umbrella stand, glue the blue Italian pottery with the blue flower and green leaves. Next, glue pieces of floral cup handles to the upper right and lower left of the Italian pottery. Variously position the white scalloped plate shards around the piece of Italian pottery that you have already glued. When these are glued, attach the two remaining blue-and-white chopstick holders into place—one to the left of the Italian pottery and one to the right, almost to the base border. When these are in place, glue the blue-and-green ceramic lid with blue knob next to the chopsticks holder that is located to the left of the Italian pottery piece. Glue the white ceramic lid to the right of the other chopstick holder.

Once these key pieces are in place, turn your attention to the back center of the umbrella stand. Glue the bone and white chopstick holders in an upside down and angled T position. With the mastic and craft stick, put glue on the blue bird and place it just below the T. The fish goes to the right of the bird and slightly lower down so its tail almost touches the bottom base border. When all these pieces are anchored, randomly glue the remaining shards to fill in empty space. Don't forget to place buttons and old coins, marbles and mirrors, and bits of colored glass wherever you think they would look best. The idea is to create visual interest in terms of texture and color patterns, while at the same time making sure that your piece works as a unified whole.

4 Apply the Grout

Put masking tape around the inside mouth of the base. This will ensure that excess grout doesn't ruin the look of the inside mouth of the umbrella stand. With particle mask on, pour about 2 cups (500 ml) of mauve grout into a disposable container. Adding a little water at a time, mix with a craft stick until it is thoroughly mixed to the consistency of peanut butter. Put the rubber or latex gloves on and place a handful of grout onto the umbrella stand, rubbing it into all cracks and crevices. Continue until the surface of the umbrella stand is entirely covered in grout.

Dampen the sponge and begin wiping away the excess grout. Resist pulling the umbrella stand toward you as tilting it may pop off pieces of china or grout. When all excess grout has been removed, gently wipe each and every piece attached to the stand. When the grout has dried, remove the tape and discard. For gift-giving, your project needs little more than a festive ribbon and a gift card.

Gallery

The purpose of this section is to provide a window into some of the most beautiful *pique assiette* art being created today. If you've made one or more of the projects outlined in this book, you likely have mastered a degree of skill and knowledge about the art form. If you have enjoyed the process up to this point, get ready for even more inspiration as you view some stunning works of art created by professionals who have been working in *pique assiette* for some time.

Banish any thought that you can't create something just as equally beautiful as the artwork in the following pages. Every one of these artists started at the beginning at some point in their careers. Don't feel daunted or intimidated as you view the projects created by these, your fellow artists. Rather, view these pieces as you would any art. Notice how each project is unique, whether steps or stepping-stones. Each artist has a distinctive style, and each piece is different from the others because it represents the vision of that artist. Focus on the unique elements as well as those that are similar. Analyze how the projects are put together. What elements are dominant? Consider why the artist chose the materials used. For example, artist Kitty Wells says she likes to "pay attention to the reflective qualities of materials and enjoys working with a combination of matte, shiny, iridescent, and reflective elements." Study how the materials the artist used were integrated into a whole. Which of these artistic creations attracts you most? Ask yourself, what does each piece of artwork inspire me to create? Then, hold fast to your vision as you birth your own ideas.

Title: Maddie, Vanna, and Gramma's Tea Table

Details: Child's tea table

Artist: Meera Lester

Description: A small table, rescued from an almost certain trip to the dump and restored with white paint, is the base for a top made of shards of porcelain espresso cups, saucers, and a child's tea set. The centerpiece, a tiny ceramic bowl found in a California antique shop, is permanently mounted to hold ginger snaps or jelly beans. Tables intended for children's furniture, provided they have a flat surface, can be easily covered with a heavy sheet of glass that has been cut to fit the top and that has had its edges sanded smooth. The glass will protect the surface art.

Title: *Le Plaisir du Jardin* (The Pleasure Garden)

Details: terra-cotta pot, 10" (25 cm), mixed media

Artist: Meera Lester

Description: This terra-cotta garden pot is transformed by the addition of mirror, china shards, pottery bits, ceramic birds, buttons, flat-sided marbles, ceramic flowers, colored pieces of glass, and found objects. It sits on terra-cotta kneeling angels that have been sprayed gold. Inspiration for the pot is attributed to trips to France and the gorgeous colors of Provence so widely appreciated in textiles and pottery. Pots like this one can evoke a sense of time and place when colors and images correlate to a particular locale.

Title: Untitled

Details: 6" (15 cm) clay pot

Artist: Nori Dolan

Description: Tiled with miscellaneous shards of dishware and tiles, the unique part of this pot is the color of the grout—turquoise—which is unexpected and lively.

Title: Makeup Mirror, Clock, and Caddies

Details: Collection of objects for a vanity, mirror, 20" (51 cm) round

Artist: Sue King

Description: All the pieces in this collection were created around the common theme of florals. The artist used numerous miscellaneous floral patterned plates and opalescent glass tiles for a shimmering effect.

Title: French-Themed Collection

Details: Assorted garden objects, both clay pots are 6" (15 cm); *Bonjour* sign is 8" × 15" (20 cm × 38 cm)

Artists: Marsha Janda-Rosenberg, Meera Lester

Description: This collection represents a French-themed collection of *pique assiette* art: *Bonjour* cement stepping-stone, clay saucer with hand-cut pear, a blue-and-yellow "cup" and saucer from clay, a blue-and-white sphere, and a tile-rimmed blue glazed pot. The sunflowers and dried lavender evoke the ambience of a warm afternoon in Avignon.

Title: Fine Wine

Details: Wine, grapes, and glasses wall plaque, 13" × 18" (33 cm × 46 cm)

Artist: Marsha Janda-Rosenberg

Description: This vineyard *pique assiette* plaque portrays a love of fine wine and features hand-cut clay wine bottle, glasses, grapes, and grape leaves. If food and wine motifs are appealing to you, try incorporating images into your *pique assiette* art of regional foods, favorite cheeses or breads, and/or foreign phrases for cooking, eating, or imbibing.

Title: Vintage Magazine Table in Pastels

Details: Vintage magazine table with *pique assiette* top in pastels

Artist: Marsha Janda-Rosenberg

Description: Pink English plates, china with mint swirls, yellow accent shards, and turquoise flat-sided marbles combine for a pastel look on the top of this vintage magazine table.

Title: 1950s–1960s Magazine Table with *Pique Assiette* Top

Details: Mint-colored magazine table, 22" × 27" × 13" (56 cm × 69 cm × 33 cm)

Artist: Marsha Janda-Rosenberg

Description: Assorted vintage plates were used to evoke a sense of nostalgia. In her use of undulating swirls and circles of coral, jade, mint, and cream colors, the artist has created a feeling of movement and energy. Try using vintage plates to create a retro or an Art Deco, Art Nouveau, or Arts and Crafts look. Allow other periods in time and other design styles inspire you to create unusual pieces such as this one.

Title: Untitled

Details: Clay flowerpot tiled in 1950s and 1960s floral plates

Artist: Marsha Janda-Rosenberg

Description: The floral plates the artist used are from the 1950s and 1960s and feature pink and mint trim. The inner rim of the pot is also tiled in the pink and mint colors. Perfect in a garden room, this stunning pot evokes a feeling of leisurely days of a bygone era.

Title: Spring Burstin' Out

Details: Cement border, 10" × 6" (25 cm × 15 cm)

Artist: Marsha Janda-Rosenberg

Description: The artist took an ordinary scalloped, cement tree border and embellished it with objects to give it dimension, including a miniature piano and platter, a slice of cake, frame, vase, cup, and chopstick holder. If you like elements in projects like this one to conform thematically to the place the project will live, try finding miniature garden or farm implements, toy tractors, tiny shovels, watering cans, and the like. Or, think about music, poetry, and writing in a garden and allow your imagination to direct you toward objects linked to those subjects.

Title: Untitled

Details: Plaque of hand-cut clay shapes, 15" × 24" (38 cm × 61 cm)

Artist: Marsha Janda-Rosenberg

Description: These pieces are made almost exclusively from hand-cut clay shapes.

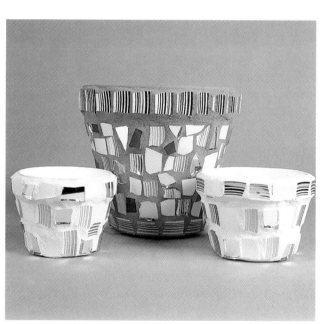

Title: New Year's Eve Stripes Galore

Details: Striped pots — three clay pots in varying sizes

Artist: Marsha Janda-Rosenberg

Description: These three clay pots are covered in unusual silver-and-white striped dish shards and broken pieces of mirror and white plates. The artist used gray-and-white grout.

Title: Untitled

Details: Decorative vase, 12" (30 cm)

Artist: Gabrielle Coppel

Description: The beauty of this vase is enhanced by the addition of fuchsia and olive green shards of china and trimmed with gold-rimmed china pieces. The choice of colors is excellent. Fuchsia is an intense version of red-violet, while olive, directly opposite on the color wheel, combines to create a complementary relationship. Gold harmonizes with both.

Title: Fallen Angel

Details: 4' × 4' (1.2 m × 1.2 m) plaque in mixed media

Artist: Kitty Wells

Description: The image of this angel was created from broken ceramic antique figurines and antique plate shards, residential and industrial tile, and broken stained glass and mirror. The angel, who is crying, represents the transmutation of pain through beauty. Allow angel iconography or masks of other cultures to pique your imagination and inspire you to create expressive and unique pieces such as this one.

Title: Celebration of Nature

Details: 4' (1.2 m) design on plywood with mirror, tile, and concrete

Artist: Kitty Wells

Description: This project is a communal piece created by the artist and her girlfriends in the traditional tree of life motif. For inspiration, look to ancient and modern symbols that express your views about the world, spirituality, community, culture, and/or art.

Title: Blue Angel

Details: 4' × 4' (1.2 m × 1.2 m) plaque covered with industrial and residential tile, concrete, and shards from plates and mirrors

Artist: Kitty Wells

Description: The artist creates a self-portrait in this piece inspired by images of saints. Here the artist endeavors to bring just such an image into the modern world without making it religious. This image is crying and, like Fallen Angel, also represents the transmutation of pain through beauty. Find inspiration through religious iconography and modernize the image or look for ancient motifs that are pleasing and tailor them to suit your purpose.

Title: Steps I

Details: Risers/steps, ceramic figurines, china shards, tile

Artist: Anne Spoon-Kanner

Description: The combination of motifs, including a flower, a turtle, a bird, and other objects contribute to a pleasing textural effect. The colors of these steps undoubtedly brighten up even the foggiest days for this little house located in a California seaside town.

Title: Steps II

Details: Risers/steps, china shards, glass marbles, ceramic figures

Artist: Anne Spoon-Kanner

Description: The artist chose to adorn the risers of the steps to her 1,000-square-foot (92.9 square m) seaside cottage in primary colors (yellow and blue) and the accent colors of green and pink. She used a variety of materials for her *pique assiette* adornment, including broken plate shards, tile, and ceramic objects. The use of these colors and the alternation of round and square forms on the risers render a pleasing, welcoming effect.

Title: Steps III

Details: Risers/steps, ceramic figurines, china

Artist: Anne Spoon-Kanner

Description: These risers to a seaside cottage are adorned with shards of broken plates, glass marbles, tile, and ceramic objects. The use of the frog contributes a charming dimensional element.

Title: Amrita Fountain

Details: Outdoor fountain made of several types of tile and broken mirror shards

Artist: Kitty Wells

Description: This fountain incorporates the use of broken Tiffany glass, some 1950s tile, mirror, and some swimming pool tile. Fountains serve as wonderful bases for *pique assiette* mosaics. Be imaginative and playful, combining colorful fish tile with whimsical images or plan a more traditional design that might incorporate garden motifs or water images.

Title: Celtic Stool

Details: Three-legged stool with tile, Celtic imagery

Artist: Nori Dolan

Description: This beautiful stool combines the earth tones of browns and golds with Celtic-inspired tile for a stunning look.

Title: Untitled

Details: Terra-cotta pots on a fence

Artist: Anne Spoon-Kanner

Description: Dimensional flowers adorn these terra-cotta wall pockets as if the pockets themselves are blooming. This piece would add a spot of whimsy and color to any garden fence or wall.

Title: Untitled

Details: Foundation art on the side of a seaside cottage, approximately 7 to 8 feet (2.1 m to 2.4 m)

Artist: Anne Spoon-Kanner

Description: The cement foundation of a seaside cottage served as the base for *pique assiette* mosaic made from pink mermaids, a string of pearls, cup handles and saucers, and pink dishes. The gas meter along the cottage wall was also painted pink and the surrounding green succulents and plants complement the pink color.

Title: Semi-Demi

Details: Semi-demi, mosaic tiles

Artists: Rebecca Dennis, Paula Funt

Description: The Canadian sisters who are the artists say that this unusual piece "actually came from the family closets where the rounded doors and storage capabilities added another dimension." The repetitive nature of the motif and use of minute mosaic tiles combine to make this piece a classic item in the artisans' collection.

Chair, mixed media

Title: Gardener's Chair

Artists: Rebecca Dennis, Paula Funt

Description: Believing that every piece must portray dimension and have focal points of detail, the artists chose to combine *pique assiette* adornment on this chair with finials. In so doing, they have achieved an exquisite artistic uniqueness in their furniture creation that can't be found anywhere else.

Title: Jeremiah Filmmaker Wall

Details: Wall, tile, and mirror

Artist: Isaiah Zagar

Description: This one-of-a-kind wall art utilizes tile and mirror mosaic to accomplish the artist's vision.

Title: Patio Wall Detail at 609 S. Alder Street

Details: Patio wall mosaic detail

Artist: Isaiah Zagar

Description: This patio wall, located at 609 S. Alder Street in Philadelphia, was completed in 1991 and is a fine example of large-scale, mixed-media mosaic work.

Title: Wall at 324 Kater Street

Details: Mosaic detail

Artist: Isaiah Zagar

Description: Detail from mosaic wall art at 324 Kater Street in Philadelphia. Completed in 1999.

Title: Wall at 609 S. Alder Street

Details: Wall art, mixed media

Artist: Isaiah Zagar

Description: Work on this wall in Philadelphia was completed in 2002 and serves as a fine example of large-scale, mixed-media mosaic work.

Title: Untitled

Details: Stepping-stone with blue-and-yellow plate shards, 12" × 12" (30 cm × 30 cm)

Artist: Marsha Janda-Rosenberg

Description: By breaking a dinner plate and dividing it into four sections, the artist was able to create four corner curves. She reassembled the center of the plate in the center of the stepping-stone. Golden yellow shards were used to divide the blue plate from the yellow.

Title: Detail of Isaiah Zagar Studio Roof Deck, 1020 South Street, Philadelphia

Details: Mixed media mosaic

Artist: Isaiah Zagar

Description: Mixed-media mosaic detail.

Title: Portrait of Ferdinand Chavol

Details: Mosaic depiction of Ferdinand Chavol

Artist: Isaiah Zagar

Description: A uniquely expressive work by the same artist who creates wall art on a grand scale in and around Philadelphia. Allow this type of work to inspire you to create on a grander scale.

Title: Untitled

Details: Garden mirror, 8" × 8" (20 cm × 20 cm)

Artist: Marsha Janda-Rosenberg

Description: Around a mirror in a white frame, blue strawberries were re-created for a pleasing image. Leaf motifs were placed in the corners.

Title: Yellow Table with Vintage Plates

Details: Table, 16" × 24" (41 cm × 61 cm)

Artist: Nancy Howells

Description: This darling little accent table was first painted yellow, then adorned with vintage plates along with a knife and a spoon. This is a perfect example of how one might use collected, inherited, hand-me-down, or purchased dishware to create a beautiful piece of accent furniture.

Title: High Heels

Details: High heels, mixed media

Artist: Nancy Howells

Description: This beautiful pair of shoes is shown on black fabric with a rear mirror to reveal the mosaic work on the back of the shoes. The artist used mainly glass tiles and pieces of ceramic fruit and vegetables from Mexico.

Resources

SUPPLIERS

Dick Blick Art Materials

www.dickblick.com

This site offers for sale supplies, including mosaic adhesives, cements, grouts, mosaic kits, projects, molds, tools, accessories, videos, books, and CD-ROMs.

diMosaico

www.dimosaico.com

For artists interested in using stone or tesserae in their creations, this company carries stone harvested from quarries all over the world. In addition, artists will find tools and other supplies, including rare smalti and marble. This site is an excellent resource for those interested in the art of Roman mosaic.

Home Depot

www.homedepot.com

Home Depot is found in major cities throughout the United States and carries tools for working with tile, a variety of tiles and grouts in many colors, backer board and other underlayments, adhesives, sponges, gloves, and books.

Just Glass

A Division of Safe House of Southeast Wisconsin, Inc.

www.justglass.org/mosaic.htm

This resource provides adhesives, books, glass chips, grout, stepping-stone kits, molds, forms, and much more.

KPTiles — Mosaic Tile Supplies

www.KPTiles.com

This company specializes in offering dozens of hand-cut mosaic tiles and china pieces from classic transferware to chintz patterns. It also sells sea glass, vitreous glass, and tiles in the shapes of heart, leaves, and sea creatures.

Mosaic Elements.Com

www.mosaicelements.com

This site offers handmade, creative ceramic shapes that will enhance mosaic and pique assiette projects.

Mosaic Matters

www.mosaicmatters.co.uk

An online magazine for all things mosaic.

MosaicMercantile.com

www.mosaicmercantile.com

This site refers to itself as the "world's premier wholesale source" and its myriad offerings include mosaic tile, forms, kits, tools, grout, adhesives, and books, as well as links and a search feature that allows individuals to find the retail source nearest them that carries MosaicMercantile products.

Monster Mosaic Supplies

www.monstermosaics.com

This company sells mosaic supplies, including tiles, grout, smalti, mirror frames, tesserae, and other items.

Society of American Mosaic Artists (SAMA)

www.americanmosaics.org/supplies

This site includes an extensive list of suppliers—all of them members of SAMA. Included in the listings are site locations and phone and fax numbers.

The China Detectives

www.chinadectectives.freeserve.co.uk/index.htm
Based in the United Kingdom, this company is a leading European matching and replacement service for discontinued tableware, china, pottery, and stoneware. It also offers broken china shards for sale by weight.

Wits End Mosaics

www.mosaics-witsend.com
This site offers books, tools, micro-mosaics, mesh, unglazed porcelain, smalti, and other supplies, as well as online instructions, and an art gallery.

BIBLIOGRAPHY

Cunningham, Jo. *The Collector's Encyclopedia of American Dinnerware*. Values updated 1998. Paducah: Collector Books, 1982.

Ling, Roger. *Ancient Mosaics*. Princeton: Princeton University Press, 1998.

Locktov, JoAnn, and Leslie Plummer Claggett. *The Art of Mosaic Design, A Collection of Contemporary Artists*. Gloucester: Rockport Publishers, Inc., Quarry Books, 1998.

Marshall, Marlene Hurley. *Making Bits and Pieces Mosaics, Creative Projects for Home & Garden*. Pownal: Storey Books, 1998.

Mastandrea, Doreen. *Mosaics Inside & Out, Patterns and Inspirations for 17 Mosaic Projects*. Gloucester: Rockport Publishers, Inc., Quarry Books, 2001.

Rinker, Harry L., *Dinnerware of the 20th Century: The Top 500 Patterns*. New York: Random House, House of Collectibles, Crown Publishing Group, 1997.

Sheerin, Connie. *Mosaics in an Afternoon*. New York: Sterling Publishing Co., Inc., 2000.

Von Schaewen, Deidi, and John Maizels. *Fantasy Worlds*. Bonn: Taschen, 1999.

Wills, Margaret Sabo. *Decorating with Tile*. Upper Saddle River: Creative Homeowner, 2000.

WEB SOURCES

These Web sites serve as points of departure for inspiration and information about mosaics and, in particular, *pique assiette* mosaics. They may include some or all of the following: newletters, links, books, visual images, galleries, class listings, professional association listings, and additional resources.

www.americanmosaics.org

www.bamm.org.uk

www.bamm.org.uk/australasia/
mosaic_association_of_australia.htm

www.gardenmosaics.com

www.mosaicdesigns.net

www.mosaicmatters.com

www.rawvision.com

www.smashingchina.com

www.thejoyofshards.co.uk

www.mosaicmatters.co.uk

Directory of Contributors

Gabrielle Coppel
4330 Bain Avenue
Santa Cruz, CA 95062
831-462-5379

Nori Dolan
Pieces of My Heart
P.O. Box 7294
Santa Cruz, CA 95061
831-457-2043

Rachel Dennis & Rebecca Funt
74 Industry Street
Toronto, Ontario
Canada M6M 4I7
416-787-5526
www.mosaicwares.com

Emily Hammergren
1335 Brommer Street
Santa Cruz, CA 98062
831-464-8731
www.dishfunctionalart.com

Nancy Howells
421 Gharkey Street
Santa Cruz, CA 95060
www.paintedchairstudio.com
831-425-1602

Theresa Janda
220 Jasmine Lane
Watsonville, CA 95076

Marsha Janda-Rosenberg
4841 Cherryvale Avenue
Soquel, CA 95073
831-462-9900
www.mosaicelements.com
marsha@mosaicelements.com

Sue King
75 Cutter Drive
Watsonville, CA 95076

Meera Lester
5264 Romford Drive
San Jose, CA 95124
408-264-1045
meeraL@aol.com

Anne Spoon-Kanner
501 Beverly Avenue
Capitola, CA 95010
831-476-2259
annekanner@baymoon.com

Kitty Wells
351 West Oakwood Boulevard
Redwood City, CA 94061
kittyw@webcastcentral.com

Jennifer Wills, photographer
www.oceanexposures.com
Jwills@oceanexposures.com

Isaiah Zagar
826 South Street
Philadelphia, PA 19147

About the Author

Meera Lester is an internationally published writer based in San Jose, California, where she writes books, articles, novels, short stories, and screenplays. Her last book, *Writing for the Ethnic Markets*, was purchased by the U.S. Information Service for libraries abroad. When she isn't writing, Meera enjoys oil painting, gardening, and creating *pique assiette* mosaics.

About the Artist

Marsha Janda-Rosenberg is a ceramic and *pique assiette* artist. She often incorporates her own handmade clay pieces into her projects. Her work can be found at art shows and galleries in California, and she can be reached at marsha@mosaicelements.com

Acknowledgments

Dedicated to the memory of Steve. Your light will always illuminate my life.

Thanks to Paula Munier for her vision and incredible sense of timing and to Mary Ann Hall for her ability to shepherd this project from start to finish with infinite patience and grace. I'm grateful to artist and fellow contributor Marsha Janda-Rosenberg and photographer extraordinaire Jennifer Wills for their hard work on this project.

Huge hugs and thanks go to my girlfriends Anita Llewellyn and Kathryn Makris for their encouragement and enduring faith in my vision and creativity. A giant thank you to teacher and fellow artist Kay Nichols for sharing with me her incredible grasp of the world of color and form.

To my Thursday night writing friends to whom I'll always be indebted for the brutal honesty, sincere feedback, and ongoing support over the years, and to my Tuesday night art friends with whom I'll paint or create mosaics until my dying day, I'd like to say thank you and never give up. Whether it's writing or art, it can always be rewritten, re-created, or recycled.

To Sandy Cressman, Pat Paquette, and Susan Reynolds, I offer my gratitude for your help with French translation and photography issues.

I wish to thank my son Joshua Solomon Lester for his outstanding technical support. For their unconditional love and belief in me, I wish to thank my daughter Heather Pomeroy, her husband Aaron, and their twins, Madison Rose and Savannah Michelle. Hugs and thanks also go to Nandini Garud, Leeanna Franklin, and Becky Cahoon, who spirited me away when I needed it most and showed me how to be a really true friend and artist.

Finally, a very special thanks to all contributing artists for opening their homes and studios and sharing their beautiful works of art.

— Meera Lester

I would like to thank my husband Michael and daughters Lindsey and Lauren for their love and creative inspiration. I would also like to thank my dear friend and partner Christine Larice-Zapata for her ongoing support and helpfulness. I would also like to acknowledge my coauthor Meera Lester and photographer Jennifer Wills for making the creative process in producing this book such a wonderful and fun experience.

— Marsha Janda-Rosenberg